Betty Crocker's

EASY BREAKFASTS AND BRUNCHES

PRENTICE HALL

New York   London   Toronto   Sydney   Tokyo   Singapore

PRENTICE HALL
15 Columbus Circle
New York, New York, 10023

Library of Congress Cataloging-in-Publication Data

Crocker, Betty.
    [Easy breakfasts and brunches]
    Betty Crocker's Easy breakfasts and brunches.
        p.   cm.
    Includes index.
    ISBN 0-671-88772-6
    1. Breakfasts. 2. Brunches. I. Title. II. Title:
Easy breakfasts and brunches.
TX733.C76   1994
641.5'2—dc20   93-32577
                                                    CIP

Manufactured in the United States of America

10 9 8 7 6 5 4 3 2 1

First Edition

Contents

Introduction

—■—

After a busy week, a relaxing breakfast is a perfect way to start the weekend. Whether you prefer breakfast classics such as fluffy omelets, piping hot waffles, and oven-fresh coffee cakes, or want to explore new adventures in breakfast, you'll love this book.

We've collected some of the most appealing—and easy to prepare—breakfast ideas that are sure to inspire you when you'd like to entertain as well as give you ideas for everyday breakfasts and brunches.

Looking for a main dish? Try Breakfast Potato Casserole, Herbed Eggs and Vegetables on Polenta or Homespun Sausage Pie. Hungry for breakfast treats hot off the griddle? Then you'll enjoy Applesauce Pancakes, Raspberry Crepes and New Orleans French Toast.

Who can resist fresh baked goods in the morning? Serve Blueberry-Streusel Muffins, French Breakfast Puffs, Buttermilk Biscuits or Poppy Seed-Walnut Coffee Cake, and no one will be late for breakfast! And when you're ready for more than just orange juice and coffee, you'll enjoy Grapefruit Juleps, Cafe Mexicano and Orange Salad with Pecan Dressing.

We have also included a whole section of how to cook eggs just the way you like them as well as information on how to make perfect coffee and tea. We know you'll agree that this is just the book for when you want to wake up and smell the coffee!

THE BETTY CROCKER EDITORS

Breakfast and Brunch Basics

ALL ABOUT EGGS

Eggs are a favorite at breakfast and brunch, and the following recipes will give you all the information you'll need to make your favorite egg dishes.

Soft-Cooked Eggs

You can cook any number of eggs at one time, even combine cooking soft- and hard-cooked eggs.

Place egg(s) in saucepan. Add enough cold water to come at least 1 inch above eggs. Heat rapidly to boiling; remove from heat. Cover and let stand 3 minutes. Immediately cool eggs in cold water several seconds to prevent further cooking. Cut eggs in half. Scoop eggs from shells.

Hard-Cooked Eggs

Hard-cooked eggs are always good to have on hand for quick lunches and garnishes. Use a crayon to mark hard-cooked eggs before refrigerating. Have an unmarked egg? Spin it—if the egg wobbles instead of spinning, it is uncooked.

Place egg(s) in saucepan. Add enough cold water to come at least 1 inch above eggs. Heat rapidly to boiling; remove from heat. Cover and let stand 18 minutes. Immediately cool eggs in cold water to prevent further cooking. Tap egg to crackle shell. Roll egg between hands to loosen shell, then peel. If shell is hard to peel, hold egg in cold water.

Poached Eggs

Be sure to use a pan large enough to accommodate all the eggs you want to poach at one time. They shouldn't touch while cooking.

Heat water (1½ to 2 inches) to boiling; reduce to simmering. Break each egg into custard cup or saucer. Hold cup or saucer close to water's surface and slip egg into water. Cook about 5 minutes or until whites are set and yolks are thickened. Remove eggs with slotted spoon.

TO MICROWAVE: Microwave 2 tablespoons water in 6-ounce microwavable custard cup uncovered on high 30 to 60 seconds or until boiling. Carefully break egg into custard cup. Prick egg yolk several times with wooden pick. Cover tightly and microwave on medium (50%) 1 minute to 1 minute 30 seconds or until egg is set and yolk is thickened. Let stand covered 1 minute.

EGGS POACHED IN BROTH: Substitute chicken or beef broth for the water.

Fried Eggs

Heat margarine, butter or bacon fat (⅛ inch deep) in heavy skillet over medium heat. Break each egg into custard cup or saucer. Slip egg carefully into skillet. Immediately reduce heat to low.

Cook 5 to 7 minutes, spooning margarine over eggs, until whites are set, a film forms over yolks and yolks are thickened. Or gently turn eggs over after 3 minutes and cook 1 to 2 minutes longer or until yolks are thickened.

REDUCED-FAT FRIED EGGS: Heat just enough margarine, butter or bacon fat to coat skillet. Cook eggs over low heat about 1 minute or until edges turn white. Add 2 teaspoons water for each egg, decreasing amount slightly for each additional egg. Cover and cook 5 minutes longer or until a film forms over yolks and yolks are thickened.

Scrambled Eggs

Scrambled eggs shouldn't brown—reduce heat immediately if they start to.

> **2 eggs**
> **2 tablespoons milk, cream or water**
> **¼ teaspoon salt**
> **Dash of pepper**
> **1½ teaspoons margarine or butter**

Stir eggs, milk, salt and pepper thoroughly with fork for a uniform yellow, or slightly for streaks of white and yellow. Heat margarine in 8-inch skillet over medium heat just until hot enough to sizzle a drop of water. Pour egg mixture into skillet.

As mixture begins to set at bottom and side, gently lift cooked portions with spatula so that thin, uncooked portion can flow to bottom. Avoid constant stirring. Cook 3 to 4 minutes or until eggs are thickened throughout but still moist.

TO MICROWAVE: Microwave margarine uncovered on high in 1-quart microwavable casserole or 4-cup microwavable measure about 30 seconds or until melted. Stir in eggs, milk, salt and pepper. Microwave uncovered 1 minute 30 seconds to 2 minutes, stirring with fork after 1 minute, until eggs are puffy and set but still moist. Stir before serving.

FANCY SCRAMBLED EGGS: For each serving, stir in 2 tablespoons of one or more of the following: shredded Cheddar, Monterey Jack or Swiss cheese; chopped mushrooms; snipped chives; snipped parsley; crisply cooked and crumbled bacon;* finely shredded dried beef;* chopped fully cooked smoked ham.*

*Omit salt.

French Omelet

2 teaspoons margarine or butter
2 eggs, beaten

Heat margarine in 8-inch omelet pan or skillet over medium-high heat just until margarine begins to brown. As margarine melts, tilt pan to coat bottom.

Quickly pour eggs into pan. Slide pan back and forth rapidly over heat and, at the same time, quickly stir with fork to spread eggs continuously over bottom of pan as they thicken. Let stand over heat a few seconds to brown bottom of omelet lightly. (Do not overcook—omelet will continue to cook after folding.)

Tilt pan and run fork under edge of omelet, then jerk pan sharply to loosen from bottom of pan. Fold portion of omelet nearest you just to center. (Allow for portion of omelet to slide up side of pan.) Turn omelet onto warm plate, flipping folded portion of omelet over so far side is on bottom. Tuck sides of omelet under if necessary.

TO MICROWAVE: Place margarine in microwavable pie plate, 9 × 1¼ inches. Microwave uncovered on high 30 seconds or until melted. Tilt pie plate to coat bottom completely. Pour eggs into pie plate. Elevate pie plate on inverted microwavable dinner plate in microwave. Cover with waxed paper and microwave 2 minutes to 2 minutes 30 seconds, moving cooked outer edge of omelet to center and gently shaking pie plate to distribute uncooked egg after 1 minute, until center is set but still moist.

FAVORITE FRENCH OMELET: Fold in one or more of the following:

2 tablespoons shredded Cheddar, Monterey Jack, Swiss or blue cheese
2 tablespoons chopped mushrooms
2 tablespoons chopped chives or parsley
2 tablespoons crisply cooked and crumbled bacon, finely shredded dried beef or chopped fully cooked ham
1 tablespoon canned chopped green chiles

1. Tilt pan and run fork under edge of omelet, then jerk skillet sharply to loosen eggs from bottom of skillet. Fold portion of omelet just to center.

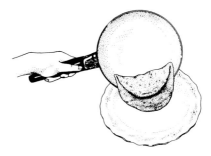

2. Turn omelet onto plate, flipping folded portion of omelet over so it is on the bottom.

Safe Handling and Storage of Eggs

Recently, raw eggs contaminated with salmonella bacteria have caused some outbreaks of illness. Scientists suspect salmonella can be transmitted from infected laying hens directly into the interior of the eggs before the shells are formed. People who are particularly vulnerable to salmonella infections include the very young, the elderly, pregnant women (because of risk to the fetus) and people already weakened by serious illness or whose immune systems are weakened. Proper storage and cooking of eggs is necessary to prevent the growth of potentially harmful bacteria. For more information on handling eggs safely, call the USDA Meat and Poultry Hotline at 1-800-535-4555.

• Purchase eggs from a refrigerated case and refrigerate at a temperature no higher than 40° immediately on arriving home. You don't need to wash eggs before storing or using them because this is routine in commercial egg processing.

• Look for eggshells that are clean and not cracked. If a shell cracks between the market and home, use the egg as soon as possible in a fully cooked dish.

• Store fresh eggs in their carton to help prevent absorption of refrigerator odors. Storing eggs point down helps center the yolk, resulting in more attractive hard- and soft-cooked eggs.

• Wash hands, utensils, equipment and work areas with hot, soapy water before and after they come in contact with eggs and dishes where eggs are a main ingredient, such as quiches.

• Avoid keeping eggs at room temperature for more than two hours, including time for preparing and serving (not including cooking). If hard-cooked eggs are hidden for an egg hunt, either follow the two-hour rule or don't eat the eggs.

• Refrigerate raw and cooked eggs. Use raw eggs in the shell within five weeks and hard-cooked eggs (in the shell or peeled) within one week. Use leftover raw yolks and whites within two days. Unbroken egg yolks store best when covered with a small amount of water.

Cooking with Eggs

• Avoid eating raw eggs and foods containing raw eggs. Homemade foods such as ice cream, eggnog and mayonnaise should be avoided unless the eggs in the recipes are cooked. Commercial forms of these foods are safe to serve because they contain pasteurized eggs. Pasteurization destroys salmonella bacteria.

• To measure 1 cup, depending on the size of the egg you need 4 to 6 eggs, 8 to 10 whites or 12 to 14 yolks.

• Cook eggs thoroughly until both the yolk and white are firm, not runny, to kill any bacteria that might be present.

• Keep cooking temperatures medium to low. High heat and overcooking cause egg whites to shrink and become tough and rubbery; yolks become tough and their surface may turn green. Omelets are the exception; cook them over medium-high heat.

• Serve cooked eggs and egg dishes immediately after cooking or refrigerate at once for later use. Use within two days.

• To refrigerate, divide large amounts of hot-cooked egg-rich dishes into several shallow containers so they will cool quickly.

Doneness Test

Cook eggs thoroughly until both the yolk and white are firm, not runny. For food safety reasons, we recommend an internal temperature of 145° to 150°. Cooking at low heat helps to achieve the desired internal temperature without resulting in rubbery eggs. In some recipes, eggs may be somewhat firmer than expected but these cooking times ensure that they will be safe to eat.

BEVERAGE BAR

Terrific Coffee and Tea Techniques
No time is a well-brewed eye-opener more welcome than at breakfast. Whether you prefer coffee or tea, you'll benefit from the guidelines below.

About Coffee
• Start with a thoroughly clean coffee maker. Wash after each use with hot, soapy water and rinse well with hot water; never scour with an abrasive pad. When cleaning an automatic coffee maker, follow the manufacturer's directions.

• Always use fresh coffee and freshly drawn cold water. Never use hot water, especially in automatic coffee makers; it changes percolating time.

• Serve steaming-hot coffee as soon as possible after brewing. If coffee must stand any length of time, remove grounds and hold coffee at serving temperature over very low heat.

• Keep ground coffee tightly covered.

Preparation Methods
Automatic: Follow manufacturer's directions for selecting grind of coffee (special ones are available), measuring and brewing the coffee and holding the coffee at serving temperature.

Drip: Measure cold water and heat to boiling. Preheat coffeepot by rinsing with very hot water. Measure drip-grind coffee into filter paper in cone or into filter section of coffeepot, depending on the type of drip pot used. Pour measured fresh boiling water into upper container; cover. When dripping is completed, remove upper container and filter section.

COFFEE CHART

Strength of brew	FOR EACH SERVING*	
	Ground Coffee	Water
Weak	1 level tablespoon	¾ cup
Medium	2 level tablespoons	¾ cup
Strong	3 level tablespoons	¾ cup

Best general recommendation.

Large Quantity Coffee
Measure regular-grind coffee into a clean cloth sack; fill only half full to allow for expansion of coffee and free circulation of water. (Soak and rinse sack thoroughly before filling.) Tie sack, allowing sufficient length of cord for fastening to handle of kettle.

Heat measured amount of cold water to full rolling boil; reduce heat. Tie sack to handle; submerge in water. Keep kettle over low heat. Brew, pushing sack up and down frequently for proper extraction, 6 to 8 minutes. When coffee is done, remove sack, permitting all extract to drain into kettle.

QUANTITY COFFEE CHART

People	Servings (⅔ cup each)	Ground Coffee	Water
12	23	2 cups	4 quarts
25	46	4 cups	8 quarts

NOTE: For 25 people, based on half the people using cream and sugar, you will need 1½ cups cream (1 tablespoon per cup) and ½ cup or 25 cubes sugar (1 teaspoon per cup).

About Tea
Whether you use loose tea or tea bags, the preparation method is the same:

• Start with a spotlessly clean teapot made of glass, china or earthenware. Add rapidly boiling water; allow to stand a few minutes, then pour out.

• Heat cold water to a full rolling boil.

• Add tea or bags to the warm pot, allowing 1 teaspoon of loose tea or 1 tea bag for each cup of tea desired. Pour boiling water over tea (¾ cup for each cup of tea); let stand 3 to 5 minutes to bring out the full flavor. Stir the tea once to ensure uniform strength.

• Do not judge the strength of tea by its color; you must taste it.

• Strain the tea or remove the bags. Serve with sugar and milk or lemon, if desired.

Prepare instant tea, a concentrate, according to the directions on the jar.

Iced Tea

Prepare tea as directed—except double the amount of tea. Strain tea over ice in pitcher or into ice-filled glasses.

NOTE: Tea that has been steeped too long or refrigerated will become cloudy. Pour a small amount of boiling water into tea to make clear again.

HOW TO USE NUTRITION INFORMATION

Nutrition information per serving for each recipe includes the amounts of calories, protein, carbohydrate, fat, cholesterol and sodium.

• If ingredient choices are given, the first listed ingredient is used in recipe nutrition information calculations.

• When ingredient ranges or more than one serving size is indicated, the first weight or serving is used to calculate nutrition information.

• "If desired" ingredients and recipe variations are not included in nutrition information calculations.

Menus

Family Favorites
Maple-Pecan Waffles (page 39)
Canadian Bacon
Orange Juice
Fiesta Hot Chocolate (page 76)

Company Brunch
Vegetable-Sausage Strata (page 17)
Spiced Honey-Lemon Muffins (page 53)
Fresh Fruit with French Cream (page 90)
Café au Lait (page 75)

Holiday Breakfast
Smoked Salmon Roulade (page 17)
Make-ahead Raisin Brioche (page 64)
Tropical Salad (page 79)
International Coffee (page 76)

Breakfast for the Gang
French Toast for a Crowd (page 48)
Sausages
Oatmeal Plum Coffee Cake (page 69)
Hot Spiced Cider (page 75)
Coffee (see Large Quantity Coffee, page 9)

Hearty Winter Breakfast
Ham-and-Brie–stuffed Apples (page 35)
Glazed Chocolate Oven Doughnuts (page 58)
Strawberry Orange Juice (page 73)
Tea or Coffee

Relaxed Summer Brunch
Italian Frittata (page 13)
Fresh Herb Batter Bread (page 71)
Zesty Fruit Salad (page 79)
Grapefruit Juleps (page 73)

Italian Frittata

1
Marvelous Main Dishes

Italian Frittata

An Italian frittata is an open-face omelet. It is not folded like a French omelet and the ingredients are cooked with the eggs instead of being folded inside the eggs.

7 jumbo eggs
¼ cup diced prosciutto or fully cooked
   Virginia ham (about 2 ounces)
1 tablespoon chopped fresh basil leaves
1 tablespoon chopped fresh sage leaves
1 tablespoon chopped fresh mint leaves
1 tablespoon freshly grated Parmesan
   cheese
1 teaspoon salt
½ teaspoon pepper
2 tablespoons butter or margarine
1 small onion, finely chopped (about ¼
   cup)

Beat all ingredients except butter and onion thoroughly. Heat butter in 12-inch nonstick skillet over medium-high heat. Sauté onion in butter.

Reduce heat to medium-low. Stir onion mixture into egg mixture. Pour into skillet. Cook uncovered, gently lifting edge so uncooked portion can flow to bottom, until eggs are almost set and golden brown on bottom. Place 12-inch, or larger, plate over skillet; invert omelet onto plate. Slide omelet back into skillet. Cook until eggs are set and golden brown on bottom.

6 servings

PER SERVING: Calories 145; Protein 9 g; Carbohydrate 2 g; Fat 11 g; Cholesterol 260 mg; Sodium 530 mg

Spring Vegetable Frittata

½ cup chopped onion (about 1 medium)
1 clove garlic, finely chopped
2 tablespoons margarine or butter
1 bell pepper, chopped
¼ teaspoon salt
¼ teaspoon pepper
1 small tomato, chopped
2 small zucchini, chopped
6 eggs, beaten
¼ cup grated Parmesan cheese

Heat oven to 375°. Cook and stir onion and garlic over medium-high heat in margarine in 10-inch ovenproof skillet 3 minutes. Add bell pepper; cook over medium heat about 2 minutes until crisp-tender. Add remaining ingredients except eggs and cheese; cook 4 minutes, stirring occasionally. Add eggs. Bake 10 to 12 minutes or until set in center. Sprinkle top with cheese. **6 servings**

PER SERVING: Calories 145; Protein 8 g; Carbohydrate 6 g; Fat 10 g; Cholesterol 220 mg; Sodium 260 mg

Blue Cheese Omelet with Pears

4 eggs
1 tablespoon margarine or butter
¼ cup crumbled Danish blue cheese or Gorgonzola cheese
1 tablespoon chopped chives
1 unpared pear, cut into wedges

Mix eggs with fork just until whites and yolks are blended. Heat margarine in 8-inch skillet or omelet pan over medium-high heat just until margarine begins to brown. As margarine melts, tilt skillet to coat bottom completely.

Quickly pour eggs, all at once, into skillet. Slide skillet back and forth rapidly over heat and, at the same time, stir quickly with fork to spread eggs continuously over bottom of pan as they thicken. Let stand over heat a few seconds to lightly brown bottom of omelet. (Do not overcook—omelet will continue to cook after folding.)

Tilt skillet; run fork under edge of omelet, then jerk skillet sharply to loosen eggs from bottom of skillet. Sprinkle with blue cheese and chives. Fold portion of omelet nearest you just to center. (Allow for portion of omelet to slide up side of skillet.)

Grasp skillet handle; turn omelet onto warm plate, flipping folded portion of omelet over so far side is on bottom. Serve with pear wedges. **2 servings**

PER SERVING: Calories 310; Protein 16 g; Carbohydrate 14 g; Fat 21 g; Cholesterol 440 mg; Sodium 430 mg

Blue Cheese Omelet with Pears

Smoked Fish Omelet

This omelet is a nice way to stretch the wonderful flavor of your favorite smoked fish.

6 eggs
½ cup milk
1 teaspoon all-purpose flour
⅛ teaspoon pepper
2 tablespoons margarine or butter
2 tablespoons chopped dill weed
¾ pound smoked fish
¼ cup sliced radishes

Beat eggs, milk, flour and pepper. Heat margarine in 10-inch skillet over medium heat until hot. Pour egg mixture into skillet; sprinkle with 1 tablespoon of the dill weed.

Cook until eggs are thickened throughout but still moist, 3 to 5 minutes, gently lifting edge with fork so that uncooked portion can flow to bottom. Arrange fish on eggs; place radishes in center of eggs. Sprinkle omelet with remaining dill weed. Cut into wedges to serve.

6 servings

PER SERVING: Calories 185; Protein 21 g; Carbohydrate 3 g; Fat 10 g; Cholesterol 260 mg; Sodium 550 mg

Brunch Oven Omelet

This is the perfect no-fuss breakfast for a crowd.

¼ cup (½ stick) margarine or butter
18 eggs
1 cup sour cream
1 cup milk
2 teaspoons salt
¼ cup chopped green onions (with tops)

Heat oven to 325°. Heat margarine in rectangular baking dish, 13 × 9 × 2 inches, in oven until melted. Tilt dish to coat bottom. Beat eggs, sour cream, milk and salt until blended. Stir in onions. Pour into dish.

Bake about 35 minutes or until eggs are set but moist.

12 servings

SMALL BRUNCH OVEN OMELET: Use square baking dish, 8 × 8 × 2 inches. Cut all ingredients in half. Bake about 25 minutes.

6 servings

PER SERVING: Calories 135; Protein 5 g; Carbohydrate 2 g; Fat 12 g; Cholesterol 215 mg; Sodium 470 mg

Smoked Salmon Roulade

An easy oven omelet that's rolled, quick and elegant, without the work of individual omelets.

½ cup all-purpose flour
1 cup milk
3 tablespoons chopped green onion (with tops)
1 tablespoon chopped fresh or 1 teaspoon dried dill weed
2 tablespoons margarine or butter, melted
¼ teaspoon salt
4 eggs
1 cup flaked smoked salmon*
1 package (10 ounces) frozen cut asparagus
1½ cups shredded Gruyère or Emmentaler cheese (6 ounces)

Heat oven to 350°. Line jelly roll pan, 15½ × 10½ × 1 inch, with aluminum foil. Grease foil generously. Beat flour, milk, onion, dill, margarine, salt and eggs until well blended. Pour into pan. Sprinkle with salmon. Bake 15 to 18 minutes or until eggs are set.

Meanwhile cook asparagus as directed on package; drain and keep warm. After removing eggs from oven, immediately sprinkle with cheese and asparagus. Roll up, beginning at narrow end, using foil to lift and roll roulade.

6 servings

HAM ROULADE: Substitute 1 cup coarsely chopped fully cooked smoked ham for the smoked salmon.

1 can (8 ounces) red salmon, drained and flaked, can be substituted for the smoked salmon.

PER SERVING: Calories 315; Protein 22 g; Carbohydrate 12 g; Fat 20 g; Cholesterol 220 mg; Sodium 405 mg

Vegetable-Sausage Strata

The strata is best assembled the day before—but don't bake it then. Cover and refrigerate, then bake in the morning and serve hot.

1 medium onion, chopped
1 pound pork sausage
1 loaf French bread (about 10 inches), cut into ½-inch slices
2 medium tomatoes, sliced
2 medium zucchini, sliced
½ cup ricotta cheese
¼ cup chopped fresh or 2 tablespoons dried basil leaves
6 eggs
2 cups milk

Cook onion and sausage over medium heat in 10-inch skillet 15 minutes, stirring frequently, until sausage is done; drain well. Line bottom of 2-quart round or oval baking dish with bread slices. Top bread with sausage mixture. Arrange tomato and zucchini slices over sausage mixture. Spoon cheese over vegetables; sprinkle with basil. Beat eggs in medium bowl; stir in milk. Pour over entire mixture. Cover and refrigerate at least 2 hours or overnight.

Heat oven to 350°. Bake strata uncovered 45 to 55 minutes until puffed and set in center. Serve immediately.

8 servings

PER SERVING: Calories 405; Protein 18 g; Carbohydrate 45 g; Fat 17 g; Cholesterol 190 mg; Sodium 680 mg

Rolled Ham and Gruyère Omelet

Rolled Ham and Gruyère Omelet

½ cup all-purpose flour
1 cup milk
2 tablespoons margarine or butter, melted
½ teaspoon salt
4 eggs
1 cup coarsely chopped fully cooked smoked ham
1 small onion, chopped
1½ cups shredded Gruyère or Swiss cheese (6 ounces)
1 cup chopped fresh spinach

Heat oven to 350°. Line jelly roll pan, 15½ × 10½ × 1 inch, with aluminum foil. Generously grease foil. Beat flour, milk, margarine, salt and eggs until well blended; pour into pan. Sprinkle with ham and onion.

Bake until eggs are set, 15 to 18 minutes. Immediately sprinkle with cheese and spinach; roll up, beginning at narrow end and using foil to lift and roll omelet. Arrange additional spinach leaves on serving plate if desired. Cut omelet into about 1½-inch slices.   **6 servings**

ROLLED BACON AND GRUYÈRE OMELET: Substitute 8 slices bacon, crisply cooked and crumbled, for the ham.

ROLLED SAUSAGE AND GRUYÈRE OMELET: Substitute 1 package (8 ounces) fully cooked sausage links, cut up, for the ham.

PER SERVING: Calories 300; Protein 19 g; Carbohydrate 13 g; Fat 19 g; Cholesterol 180 mg; Sodium 580 mg

Top Your Own Eggs

A fun idea for a low-key breakfast. This is nice served with Crab and Pepper Hash (page 31).

½ cup milk
¼ teaspoon pepper
10 eggs
¼ cup (½ stick) margarine or butter
Shredded Cheddar cheese
Sour cream
Chopped green chiles
Chopped fresh tomatoes

Place milk, pepper and eggs in blender; cover and blend until mixture is foamy. Heat margarine in 10-inch skillet over medium heat; pour egg mixture into skillet.

As mixture begins to set at bottom and side, gently lift cooked portions with spatula so uncooked portions can flow to bottom. Cook 3 to 5 minutes or until eggs are thickened throughout but still moist. Serve eggs with cheese, sour cream, green chiles and tomatoes.

8 servings

PER SERVING: Calories 150; Protein 8 g; Carbohydrate 2 g; Fat 12 g; Cholesterol 270 mg; Sodium 150 mg

Home-style Scrambled Eggs

Home-style Scrambled Eggs

4 eggs
3 tablespoons water
¾ teaspoon salt
¼ cup (½ stick) margarine or butter
1 cup cubed cooked potato (1 medium)
3 tablespoons finely chopped onion
1 small zucchini, halved and sliced
1 tomato, chopped

Beat eggs, water and salt with fork. Heat margarine in 10-inch skillet over medium heat until melted; cook and stir vegetables in margarine 2 minutes. Pour egg mixture into skillet.

As mixture begins to set at bottom and side, gently lift cooked portions with spatula so that thin, uncooked portion can flow to bottom. Avoid constant stirring. Cook until eggs are thickened throughout but still moist, 3 to 5 minutes.

4 servings

TO MICROWAVE: Omit margarine. Beat eggs, water and salt with fork in 1½-quart microwavable casserole. Stir in potato, onion and zucchini. Cover tightly and microwave on high, stirring every minute, until eggs are puffy and set but still moist, 4 to 5 minutes. (Eggs will continue to cook while standing.) Stir in tomato.

PER SERVING: Calories 230; Protein 7 g; Carbohydrate 12 g; Fat 17 g; Cholesterol 210 mg; Sodium 600 mg

Potatoes and Eggs

12 ounces bulk pork sausage
1 small onion, chopped
3 cups frozen shredded hash brown potatoes
1 teaspoon herb-seasoned salt
1½ cups shredded Swiss cheese (6 ounces)
6 eggs

Heat oven to 350°. Cook and stir sausage and onion in 10-inch skillet over medium heat until sausage is brown; drain. Stir in frozen potatoes and herb-seasoned salt. Cook, stirring constantly, just until potatoes are thawed, about 2 minutes. Remove from heat; stir in cheese. Spread in ungreased rectangular baking dish, 11 × 7 × 1½ inches.

Make 6 indentations in potato mixture with back of spoon; break 1 egg into each indentation. Bake uncovered until eggs are of desired doneness, 20 to 25 minutes. **6 servings**

PER SERVING: Calories 425; Protein 21 g; Carbohydrate 18 g; Fat 30 g; Cholesterol 260 mg; Sodium 1040 mg

Eggs Benedict

Hollandaise Sauce (below)
3 English muffins
Margarine or butter, softened
**6 thin slices Canadian-style bacon or
    fully cooked smoked ham**
1 teaspoon margarine or butter
6 Poached Eggs (page 6)

Prepare Hollandaise Sauce; keep warm. Split English muffins; toast. Spread each muffin half with margarine; keep warm. Cook bacon in 1 teaspoon margarine over medium heat until light brown. Prepare Poached Eggs. Place 1 slice bacon on each muffin half. Top with 1 poached egg. Spoon warm sauce over eggs.

6 servings

Hollandaise Sauce

3 egg yolks
1 tablespoon lemon juice
½ cup (1 stick) firm butter*

Stir egg yolks and lemon juice vigorously in 1½-quart saucepan. Add ¼ cup of the butter. Heat over *very low heat,* stirring constantly with wire whisk, until butter is melted. Add remaining butter. Continue stirring vigorously until butter is melted and sauce is thickened. (Be sure butter melts slowly as this gives eggs time to cook and thicken sauce without curdling.) Serve hot or at room temperature. Cover and refrigerate any remaining sauce. To serve, stir in small amount of hot water. **About ¾ cup sauce**

CRAB BENEDICT: Substitute 1½ cups chopped cooked crabmeat for the bacon. Heat in margarine just until hot.

SEAFOOD BENEDICT: Substitute 1½ cups chopped cooked mixed crabmeat, scallops, shrimp and lobster for the bacon. Heat in margarine just until hot.

Do not use margarine, butter blends or spreads in this recipe.

PER SERVING: Calories 365; Protein 15 g; Carbohydrate 8 g; Fat 30 g; Cholesterol 445 mg; Sodium 385 mg

Cooking with Eggs

• Cook eggs thoroughly until both the yolk and white are firm, not runny, to kill any bacteria that might be present.

• Keep cooking temperatures medium to low. High heat and overcooking cause egg whites to shrink and become tough and rubbery; yolks become tough and their surface may turn green. Omelets are the exception; cook them over medium-high heat.

• Serve cooked eggs and egg dishes immediately after cooking or refrigerate at once for later use. Use within two days.

• To refrigerate, divide large amounts of hot-cooked egg-rich dishes into several shallow containers so they will cool quickly.

MARVELOUS MAIN DISHES ■ 23

Eggs Florentine

When a dish is styled à la Florentine, *you may be sure that it is made with spinach. This French preparation, with a traditional Mornay Sauce (a white sauce flavored with cheese), is lovely for a late breakfast.*

1 package (10 ounces) frozen chopped spinach
Mornay Sauce (below)
4 Poached Eggs (page 6)
2 tablespoons grated Parmesan cheese
1 tablespoon dry bread crumbs

Cook spinach as directed on package; drain. Place spinach in ungreased shallow 1-quart baking dish; keep warm. Prepare Mornay Sauce and Poached Eggs. Place eggs on spinach. Cover with Mornay Sauce; Sprinkle with cheese and bread crumbs. Set oven control to broil or 550°. Broil with top about 5 inches from heat until light brown, about 1 minute.

4 servings

Mornay Sauce

2 teaspoons margarine or butter
2 teaspoons all-purpose flour
½ teaspoon chicken bouillon granules
Dash of ground nutmeg
Dash of ground red pepper (cayenne)
¾ cup half-and-half
¼ cup shredded Swiss cheese

Heat margarine in 1-quart saucepan until melted. Blend in flour, bouillon granules, nutmeg and red pepper. Cook over low heat, stirring constantly, until mixture is smooth and bubbly. Stir in half-and-half. Heat to boiling, stirring constantly. Boil and stir 1 minute. Add cheese; stir until cheese is melted.

PER SERVING: Calories 215; Protein 12 g; Carbohydrate 8 g; Fat 15 g; Cholesterol 240 mg; Sodium 220 mg

Yucatán Poached Eggs

1 small onion, chopped (about ¼ cup)
2 tablespoons margarine or butter
1 tablespoon vegetable oil
2 medium tomatoes, chopped (about 2 cups)
1 jalapeño chile, seeded and finely chopped
2 tablespoons chopped fresh cilantro
4 eggs
Salt and pepper to taste
½ cup shelled pumpkin seeds, toasted and ground

Cook and stir onion in margarine and oil in 10-inch skillet until tender. Stir in tomatoes, chile and cilantro. Cover and cook over low heat 10 minutes, stirring occasionally.

Break each egg into measuring cup or saucer; holding cup close to skillet, slip 1 egg at a time onto tomato mixture. Cover and cook until of desired doneness, 3 to 5 minutes. Season to taste with salt and pepper; sprinkle with ground pumpkin seeds. **4 servings**

PER SERVING: Calories 205; Protein 8 g; Carbohydrate 7 g; Fat 16 g; Cholesterol 210 mg; Sodium 270 mg

Herbed Eggs and Vegetables on Polenta

Polenta, a staple in northern Italy and eastern European countries, is a type of cornmeal pudding. It is also popular cooled, then sliced and fried or baked and served with other foods.

⅔ cup yellow cornmeal
½ cup cold water
2 cups boiling water
1 tablespoon chopped fresh or 1 teaspoon dried basil leaves
½ teaspoon salt
1 tablespoon reduced-calorie margarine
8 ounces small whole mushrooms
1 medium onion, sliced
1 medium red bell pepper, cut into strips
1 tablespoon chopped fresh or 1 teaspoon dried basil leaves
½ cup chicken broth
2 teaspoons cornstarch
½ teaspoon salt
6 hard-cooked eggs, cut lengthwise into halves

Mix cornmeal and cold water in 2-quart nonstick saucepan. Stir in boiling water, 1 tablespoon basil and ½ teaspoon salt. Cook, stirring occasionally, until mixture thickens and boils; reduce heat to low. Cook about 10 minutes, stirring occasionally, until very thick; remove from heat. Keep warm.

Heat margarine in 10-inch nonstick skillet over medium heat. Cook mushrooms, onion, bell pepper and 1 tablespoon basil about 7 minutes, stirring occasionally, until onion is softened. Stir broth into cornstarch and ½ teaspoon salt. Stir into vegetable mixture. Heat to boiling, stirring occasionally. Boil and stir 1 minute; reduce heat.

Carefully stir eggs into vegetable mixture. Simmer uncovered 3 to 5 minutes, without stirring, until eggs are hot. Serve over polenta.

4 servings

PER SERVING: Calories 170; Protein 6 g; Carbohydrate 28 g; Fat 4 g; Cholesterol 55 mg; Sodium 680 mg

Huevos Rancheros

Huevos Rancheros ("ranch-style eggs") in fact refers to any egg dish served on tortillas. Spicy sausage makes this version a hearty one.

8 ounces bulk chorizo sausage
Vegetable oil
6 corn tortillas (6 to 7 inches in diameter)
1¼ cups warm salsa
6 fried eggs
1½ cups shredded Cheddar cheese (6 ounces)

Cook and stir sausage until done; drain. Heat ⅛ inch oil in 8-inch skillet over medium heat just until hot. Cook tortillas, one at a time, in oil until crisp, about 1 minute; drain.

Spread each tortilla with 1 tablespoon salsa to soften. Place 1 egg on each tortilla; top each with scant tablespoon salsa, ¼ cup sausage, another tablespoon salsa and ¼ cup cheese.

6 servings

PER SERVING: Calories 520; Protein 23 g; Carbohydrate 24 g; Fat 37 g; Cholesterol 450 mg; Sodium 500 mg

Huevos Rancheros

Eggs and Spinach Casserole

We've used reduced-calorie items here, to help those watching their weight.

½ cup chopped onion (about 1 medium)
1 tablespoon reduced-calorie margarine
3 cups frozen shredded hash brown potatoes
½ teaspoon herb seasoning mix
½ teaspoon salt
1 package (10 ounces) frozen chopped spinach, thawed
½ cup shredded low-fat Swiss cheese (2 ounces)
½ cup low-fat sour cream
6 eggs

Heat oven to 350°. Cook onion in margarine in 10-inch skillet over medium heat until softened, stirring occasionally. Stir in frozen potatoes, seasoning mix, salt and spinach. Cook about 3 minutes, stirring constantly, just until potatoes are thawed. Stir in cheese and sour cream. Spread in ungreased square baking dish, 8 × 8 × 2 inches.

Make 6 indentations in potato mixture with back of spoon; break 1 egg into each indentation. Sprinkle with pepper if desired. Bake uncovered 30 to 35 minutes or until eggs are of desired doneness. **6 servings**

PER SERVING: Calories 255; Protein 12 g; Carbohydrate 24 g; Fat 12 g; Cholesterol 230 mg; Sodium 320 mg

Savory Egg Pockets

2 tablespoons margarine or butter
¼ cup chopped green bell pepper
1 small tomato, seeded and chopped (about ½ cup)
8 eggs
1 teaspoon Worcestershire sauce
¼ teaspoon salt
2 pita breads (6 inches in diameter), cut into halves and opened to form pockets
½ cup alfalfa sprouts

Heat margarine in 10-inch skillet over medium heat until melted. Cook bell pepper and tomato in margarine about 3 minutes, stirring occasionally, until bell pepper is tender. Mix eggs, Worcestershire sauce and salt. Pour into skillet.

As mixture begins to set at bottom and side, gently lift cooked portions with spatula so that thin, uncooked portion can flow to bottom. Avoid constant stirring. Cook 3 to 5 minutes or until eggs are thickened throughout but still moist. Spoon into pita breads. Top with alfalfa sprouts. **4 servings**

PER SERVING: Calories 320; Protein 17 g; Carbohydrate 27 g; Fat 16 g; Cholesterol 430 mg; Sodium 540 mg

Gruyère Puff in Mushroom Crust

Our unusual mushroom crust helps keep this innovative main dish at about 200 calories per serving, a boon for the calorie conscious.

Mushroom Crust (right)
1 small onion, sliced
2 tablespoons reduced-calorie margarine
2 tablespoons all-purpose flour
¼ teaspoon dry mustard
1 cup skim milk
1 cup shredded Gruyère cheese (4 ounces)
2 eggs, separated
1 egg white
1 tablespoon chopped fresh chives

Prepare Mushroom Crust. Reduce oven temperature to 350°. Cook onion in margarine in 1-quart nonstick saucepan over low heat about 3 minutes or until onion is softened. Stir in flour and mustard until blended; remove from heat. Stir in milk. Heat to boiling over low heat, stirring constantly. Boil and stir 1 minute; remove from heat. Stir in cheese until melted.

Beat egg whites in medium bowl until stiff but not dry. Beat egg yolks until light and lemon colored. Stir egg yolks into cheese mixture. Stir about one-fourth of the egg whites into cheese mixture. Fold cheese mixture into remaining egg whites; stir in chives. Spread in Mushroom Crust. Bake uncovered about 30 minutes or until golden brown and cracks feel dry.

6 servings

Mushroom Crust

3 cups finely chopped mushrooms (about 12 ounces)
1 large clove garlic, finely chopped
2 tablespoons reduced-calorie margarine
¼ cup dry bread crumbs
1 egg white

Heat oven to 375°. Spray pie plate, 9 × 1¼ inches, with nonstick cooking spray. Cook mushrooms and garlic in margarine in 10-inch nonstick skillet over medium heat about 5 minutes or until most of the moisture is evaporated; cool slightly. Stir in bread crumbs. Beat egg white until stiff peaks form; stir into mushroom mixture. Spread in pie plate. Bake about 10 minutes or until edge begins to brown and crust is set.

PER SERVING: Calories 220; Protein 12 g; Carbohydrate 12 g; Fat 14 g; Cholesterol 95 mg; Sodium 210 mg

Stir-fried Eggs with Mushrooms

A sunny breakfast stir-fry makes a nice change, with the earthy flavor of dried mushrooms.

**3 dried black Chinese mushrooms
2 tablespoons peanut oil
½ cup sliced green onions (with tops)
1 teaspoon finely chopped gingerroot
½ cup sliced oyster mushrooms
6 eggs, beaten
2 tablespoons rice wine (sake)
1 tablespoon soy sauce
Sesame oil**

Cover black mushrooms with warm water; let stand 20 minutes. Drain and rinse. Remove and discard stems from mushrooms. Cut mushrooms into thin strips; reserve.

Heat peanut oil in 10-inch skillet or wok until hot. Cook onions and gingerroot until tender; stir in reserved black mushrooms and oyster mushrooms. Mix eggs, wine and soy sauce; pour into skillet. As mixture begins to set at bottom and sides, gently lift cooked portions with spatula so that thin, uncooked portion can flow to bottom. Avoid constant stirring. Cook until eggs are thickened throughout but still moist, 3 to 5 minutes. Sprinkle with sesame oil; serve immediately. **4 servings**

PER SERVING; Calories 210; Protein 10 g; Carbohydrate 6 g; Fat 16 g; Cholesterol 320 mg; Sodium 360 mg

Breakfast Potato Casserole

1 package (6 ounces) hash brown potato mix*
**⅓ cup chopped onion
¼ cup chopped green bell pepper
8 slices bacon, crisply cooked and crumbled
1 can (8 ounces) whole kernel corn, drained
1½ cups shredded Cheddar cheese (6 ounces)
1 cup milk
5 eggs, beaten
½ teaspoon salt
Dash of ground red pepper (cayenne)
Paprika**

Heat oven to 350°. Cover potatoes with water and drain as directed on package—except omit salt. Spread potatoes in ungreased rectangular baking dish, 12 × 7½ × 2 inches. Top with onion, bell pepper, bacon, corn and cheese. Mix remaining ingredients except paprika. Pour over cheese. Sprinkle with paprika. Bake 35 to 40 minutes or until knife inserted in center comes out clean. **6 servings**

*3 cups frozen shredded hash brown potatoes can be substituted for the potato mix (do not thaw).

PER SERVING: Calories 350; Protein 18 g; Carbohydrate 28 g; Fat 19 g; Cholesterol 270 mg; Sodium 345 mg

Quiche Lorraine

A classic brunch dish, with two tasty variations.

Pastry for 9-inch one-crust pie
8 slices bacon, crisply cooked and crumbled
1 cup shredded natural Swiss cheese (4 ounces)
⅓ cup finely chopped onion
4 eggs
2 cups whipping (heavy) cream
¼ teaspoon salt
¼ teaspoon pepper
⅛ teaspoon ground red pepper (cayenne)

Heat oven to 425°. Prepare pastry. Ease into quiche dish, 9 × 1½ inches, or pie plate, 9 × 1¼ inches. Sprinkle bacon, cheese and onion in pastry-lined quiche dish. Beat eggs slightly; beat in remaining ingredients. Pour into quiche dish. Bake 15 minutes.

Reduce oven temperature to 300°. Bake about 30 minutes longer or until knife inserted in center comes out clean. Let stand 10 minutes before cutting. **6 servings**

CHICKEN QUICHE: Substitute 1 cup cut-up cooked chicken or turkey for the bacon and 1 teaspoon chopped fresh or ½ teaspoon dried thyme leaves for the red pepper. Increase salt to ½ teaspoon.

SEAFOOD QUICHE: Substitute 1 cup chopped cooked crabmeat, shrimp, seafood sticks or salmon for the bacon and green onion for the onion. (Pat crabmeat dry.) Increase salt to ½ teaspoon.

PER SERVING: Calories 630; Protein 16 g; Carbohydrate 18 g; Fat 55 g; Cholesterol 320 mg; Sodium 535 mg

Cheese Tips

- To shred a small amount of cheese, pull a swivel-bladed vegetable parer over the edge of firm cheese.

- For one cup of cheese, buy four ounces of natural or process cheese.

- Freeze firm cheeses in small amounts in tightly wrapped packages up to 4 months. Thaw cheese in refrigerator to prevent crumbling. Save leftover cheese bits to blend with cream for spreads and dips.

- Very soft cheese shreds more easily if first placed in the freezer for fifteen minutes. Or it can be finely chopped instead of shredded.

Ham Quiche

Cornmeal Quiche Shells (below)
⅓ cup shredded mozzarella cheese
2 tablespoons finely chopped fully
 cooked smoked ham
1 tablespoon finely chopped green onion
 (with top)
2 eggs
⅓ cup milk
¼ teaspoon salt
6 drops red pepper sauce

Heat oven to 425°. Prepare Cornmeal Quiche Shells. Sprinkle cheese, ham and onion in shells. Beat remaining ingredients with fork in small bowl. Divide equally between shells. Bake uncovered 10 minutes. Reduce oven temperature to 300°. Bake 20 to 25 minutes or until knife inserted halfway between center and edge comes out clean. **2 servings**

Cornmeal Quiche Shells

 ⅓ cup all-purpose flour
 1 tablespoon plus 1 teaspoon cornmeal
 ⅛ teaspoon salt
 1 tablespoon plus 2 teaspoons
  shortening
 5 to 6 teaspoons water

Mix flour, cornmeal and salt; cut in shortening thoroughly. Sprinkle in water, tossing with fork until all flour is moistened and pastry cleans side of bowl. Gather pastry into a ball. Divide into halves. Press each half firmly against bottom and side of an 8-ounce quiche dish or 10-ounce custard cup.

PER SERVING: Calories 355; Protein 17 g; Carbohydrate 24 g; Fat 21 g; Cholesterol 230 mg; Sodium 650 mg

Impossible Chile-Cheese Pie

2 cans (4 ounces each) chopped green
 chiles, drained
4 cups shredded Cheddar cheese (16
 ounces)
2 cups milk
4 eggs
1 cup Bisquick®

Heat oven to 425°. Grease pie plate, 10 × 1½ inches. Sprinkle chiles and cheese in pie plate. Place remaining ingredients in blender. Cover and blend on high speed about 15 seconds or until smooth. (Or beat remaining ingredients on high speed 1 minute.) Pour into pie plate. Bake 25 to 30 minutes or until knife inserted in center comes out clean. Cool 10 minutes.

8 servings

TO MICROWAVE: Do not grease pie plate. Decrease milk to 1½ cups. Prepare as directed. Elevate pie plate on inverted microwavable dinner plate in microwave oven. Microwave uncovered on medium-high (70%) 12 to 18 minutes, rotating pie plate ¼ turn every 6 minutes, until knife inserted in center comes out clean. Cool 10 minutes.

PER SERVING: Calories 320; Protein 20 g; Carbohydrate 14 g; Fat 25 g; Cholesterol 200 mg; Sodium 595 mg

Bean-Cheese Pie

¾ cup all-purpose flour
½ cup shredded Cheddar cheese (2 ounces)
1½ teaspoons baking powder
½ teaspoon salt
⅓ cup milk
1 egg, slightly beaten
1 can (15½ ounces) garbanzo beans, drained
1 can (15 ounces) kidney beans, drained
1 can (8 ounces) tomato sauce
½ cup chopped green bell pepper (about 1 small)
¼ cup chopped onion (about 1 small)
2 teaspoons chile powder
2 teaspoons fresh or ½ teaspoon dried oregano leaves
¼ teaspoon garlic powder
½ cup shredded Cheddar cheese (2 ounces)

Heat oven to 375°. Spray pie plate, 10 × 1½ inches, with nonstick cooking spray. Mix flour, ½ cup cheese, the baking powder and salt in medium bowl. Stir in milk and egg until blended. Spread over bottom and up side of pie plate. Mix remaining ingredients except ½ cup cheese. Spoon into pie plate; sprinkle with ½ cup cheese. Bake uncovered about 25 minutes or until edge is puffy and light brown. Let stand 10 minutes before cutting. **8 servings**

PER SERVING: Calories 315; Protein 18 g; Carbohydrate 40 g; Fat 11 g; Cholesterol 50 mg; Sodium 730 mg

Crab and Pepper Hash

¼ cup (½ stick) margarine or butter
¼ cup chopped green onions (with tops)
1 large red bell pepper, chopped
2 cloves garlic, crushed
1½ pounds small red potatoes, cooked, cut into fourths
½ teaspoon salt
½ teaspoon pepper
1 package (12 ounces) frozen crabmeat, thawed, drained and cartilage removed or salad-style imitation crabmeat, thawed

Heat margarine in 10-inch skillet until melted. Cook onion, bell pepper and garlic in margarine over medium heat until pepper is tender. Stir in remaining ingredients; cook about 5 minutes, stirring frequently, until hot. **8 servings**

PER SERVING: Calories 180; Protein 10 g; Carbohydrate 19 g; Fat 7 g; Cholesterol 45 mg; Sodium 320 mg

Red Flannel Hash

Red Flannel Hash

You may want to eat red flannel hash topped with a poached or fried egg—it's delicious either way.

2 cups chopped cooked corned beef brisket*
1½ cups chopped cooked potatoes (about 1½ medium)
1½ cups diced cooked beets (about 12 ounces fresh beets)**
⅓ cup chopped onion
½ teaspoon salt
¼ teaspoon pepper
¼ cup shortening
Chopped fresh parsley

Mix all ingredients except shortening and parsley in large bowl. Heat shortening in 10-inch skillet over medium heat until melted. Spread beef mixture in skillet. Cook 10 to 15 minutes, turning occasionally with wide spatula, until brown. Sprinkle with parsley.　　　**4 servings**

*1 can (12 ounces) corned beef can be substituted for the brisket.

**1 can (16 ounces) diced beets, drained, can be substituted for the cooked beets.

PER SERVING: Calories 360; Protein 14 g; Carbohydrate 18 g; Fat 26 g; Cholesterol 70 mg; Sodium 1100 mg

Crab Croissant Bake

4 large croissants, cut into ½-inch cubes, or 4 cups ½-inch cubes French bread
1 cup shredded Jarlsberg, Swiss or mozzarella cheese (4 ounces)
1 package (6 ounces) frozen crabmeat, thawed and well drained, or 6 ounces imitation crabmeat, cut into ½-inch pieces
2 green onions (with tops), sliced
1½ cups milk
3 eggs
½ teaspoon dry mustard
½ teaspoon salt

Arrange half of the croissant cubes in ungreased square baking dish, 8 × 8 × 2 inches. Sprinkle with ½ cup of the cheese, the crabmeat and onions. Arrange remaining cubes over top. Beat milk, eggs, mustard and salt. Pour over cubes. Cover and refrigerate at least 2 hours but no longer than 24 hours.

Heat oven to 325°. Bake uncovered 1 to 1¼ hours or until knife inserted in center comes out clean. Sprinkle with remaining ½ cup cheese. Bake about 2 minutes longer or until cheese melts. Serve immediately.　　　**6 servings**

PER SERVING: Calories 265; Protein 15 g; Carbohydrate 16 g; Fat 16 g; Cholesterol 205 mg; Sodium 720 mg

Sausage in Corn Bread with Salsa–Sour Cream Sauce

1 pound pork sausage links
Corn Bread (below)
½ cup shredded process sharp American cheese (2 ounces)
3 medium green onions (with tops), chopped (about ¼ cup)
Salsa–Sour Cream Sauce (right)

Heat oven to 400°. Cook sausages in 10-inch ovenproof skillet as directed on package; drain. Prepare Corn Cream as directed—except use skillet and stir in cheese and onions. Pour batter into skillet. Arrange sausages in spoke fashion on top. Bake about 20 minutes or until corn bread is golden brown. Serve in wedges with Salsa–Sour Cream Sauce.

6 to 8 servings

Corn Bread

1½ cups cornmeal
½ cup all-purpose flour*
¼ cup vegetable oil or shortening
1½ cups buttermilk
2 teaspoons baking powder
1 teaspoon sugar
1 teaspoon salt
½ teaspoon baking soda
2 eggs

Heat oven to 450°. Grease round pan, 9 × 1½ inches, square pan, 8 × 8 × 2 inches, or 10-inch ovenproof skillet. Mix all ingredients. Beat vigorously 30 seconds. Pour into pan. Bake round or square pan 25 to 30 minutes, skillet about 20 minutes or until golden brown. Serve warm.

12 pieces

Salsa–Sour Cream Sauce

2 cups prepared salsa
½ cup sour cream

Mix ingredients in 1-quart saucepan. Heat over medium heat until hot.

If using self-rising flour, decrease baking powder to 1 teaspoon and omit salt.

PER SERVING: Calories 455; Protein 17 g; Carbohydrate 27 g; Fat 31 g; Cholesterol 145 mg; Sodium 1740 mg

Homespun Sausage Pie

This pie is very pretty made with a lattice crust. If you'd like a lattice crust, use pastry for a two-crust pie.

1½ pounds bulk pork sausage
½ cup chopped onion (about 1 medium)
1 tablespoon sugar
1½ teaspoons salt
1 medium head green cabbage (1¾ pounds), cut into large chunks and cored
1 can (16 ounces) whole tomatoes, undrained
Pastry for 9-inch one-crust pie
2 tablespoons all-purpose flour
¼ cup cold water

Cook and stir sausage and onion in Dutch oven until sausage is done; drain. Stir in sugar, salt, cabbage and tomatoes. Heat to boiling; reduce heat. Cover and simmer 10 minutes.

Heat oven to 400°. Prepare pastry; shape into flattened round on lightly floured cloth-covered board. Roll to fit top of 2-quart casserole. Fold into fourths; cut slits so seam can escape.

Mix flour and water; stir into hot sausage mixture. Pour into ungreased casserole. Place pastry over top and unfold; seal pastry to edge of casserole. Bake until crust is brown, 25 to 30 minutes. **6 servings**

PER SERVING: Calories 450; Protein 15 g; Carbohydrate 32 g; Fat 29 g; Cholesterol 50 mg; Sodium 1550 mg

Ham-and-Brie–stuffed Apples

We like the mild, sweet taste of Golden Delicious apples to complement the ham and Brie.

4 large apples (about 2 pounds)
1 tablespoon margarine or butter
2 cups diced fully cooked smoked ham
1 cup soft bread crumbs
1 tablespoon chopped fresh chives
¼ teaspoon ground nutmeg
4 ounces Brie or Swiss cheese, thinly sliced or shredded
¾ cup dry white wine or apple juice

Cut apples lengthwise into halves. Core each and remove pulp, leaving ¼-inch shell. Chop apple pulp; reserve.

Heat margarine over medium-high heat in 3-quart saucepan until melted. Stir in ham, reserved apple pulp, bread crumbs, chives and nutmeg. Cook and stir about 5 minutes until hot. Stir in cheese until melted.

Heat oven to 375°. Place apples, cut sides up, in ungreased rectangular baking dish, 11 × 7 × 1½ inches. Divide filling evenly among apples. Pour wine around apples. Bake uncovered 25 to 30 minutes or until filling is light brown and apples are tender when pierced with fork. Spoon wine in dish over apples several times during baking. **4 servings**

PER SERVING: Calories 415; Protein 27 g; Carbohydrate 44 g; Fat 15 g; Cholesterol 65 mg; Sodium 1100 mg

Whole Wheat Waffles with Honey Butter (page 38)

2

From the Griddle

Waffles

Waffle irons come in many shapes and sizes, and this batter works well in all of them.

2 eggs
2 cups all-purpose or whole wheat flour
½ cup vegetable oil, margarine or butter (1 stick), melted
1¾ cups milk
1 tablespoon granulated or brown sugar
4 teaspoons baking powder
¼ teaspoon salt

Heat waffle iron. Beat eggs with hand beater in medium bowl until fluffy. Beat in remaining ingredients just until smooth. Pour batter from cup or pitcher onto center of hot waffle iron. Bake about 5 minutes or until steaming stops. Remove waffle carefully.

twelve 4-inch waffle squares (three 9-inch waffles)

CORN WAFFLES: Omit salt. Substitute 1 cup cornmeal for 1 cup of the flour and 1 can (8 ounces) cream-style corn for ¾ cup of the milk. Stir in few drops red pepper sauce.

PER SERVING: Calories 185; Protein 4 g; Carbohydrate 18 g; Fat 11 g; Cholesterol 50 mg; Sodium 210 mg

Whole Wheat Waffles with Honey Butter

2 eggs
2 cups whole wheat flour
1¾ cups milk
½ cup (1 stick) butter or margarine, melted, or vegetable oil
1 tablespoon packed brown sugar
4 teaspoons baking powder
½ teaspoon salt
Honey Butter (below)

Heat waffle iron. Beat eggs with hand beater until fluffy; beat in remaining ingredients except Honey Butter just until smooth. Pour batter onto center of hot waffle iron. Bake about 5 minutes or until steaming stops. Remove waffle carefully. Serve with Honey Butter.

twelve 4-inch waffle squares

Honey Butter

½ cup (1 stick) butter or margarine, softened
½ cup honey

Mix butter and honey until well blended.

PER SERVING: Calories 290; Protein 5 g; Carbohydrate 29 g; Fat 17 g; Cholesterol 80 mg; Sodium 350 mg

Macadamia Nut Waffles

2 cups Bisquick® Original baking mix
1 cup milk
2 eggs
2 tablespoons sugar
2 tablespoons vegetable oil
½ cup coarsely chopped macadamia nuts
Coconut Syrup (below)
½ cup coarsely chopped macadamia nuts

Heat waffle iron. Beat all ingredients except nuts and Coconut Syrup with wire whisk or hand beater until smooth. Stir in ½ cup nuts.

Pour batter onto center of hot waffle iron. Bake until steaming stops, about 5 minutes. Remove waffle carefully. Top with Coconut Syrup and sprinkle with ½ cup nuts.

twelve 4-inch waffle squares

Coconut Syrup

¾ cup cream of coconut (piña colada base)
1 cup light corn syrup

Mix cream of coconut and corn syrup. Heat if desired.

PER SERVING: Calories 325; Protein 4 g; Carbohydrate 39 g; Fat 17 g; Cholesterol 35 mg; Sodium 360 mg

Maple-Pecan Waffles

4 eggs
4 cups all-purpose flour
2 cups milk
1½ cups maple syrup
1 cup (2 sticks) margarine or butter, melted
¼ cup chopped pecans
2 tablespoons baking powder
Date Butter (below)

Heat waffle iron. Beat eggs until fluffy in large bowl; beat in remaining ingredients except Date Butter just until smooth. Pour batter from cup or pitcher onto center of hot waffle iron. Bake until steaming stops, about 5 minutes. Remove waffle carefully. Serve with Date Butter.

twenty-four 4-inch waffle squares

Date Butter

½ cup (1 stick) margarine or butter
¼ cup chopped dates

Mix margarine and dates in small bowl until well blended.

PER SERVING: Calories 270; Protein 4 g; Carbohydrate 32 g; Fat 14 g; Cholesterol 37 mg; Sodium 250 mg

Marmalade Belgian-Waffles with Orange Butter

Shortening
2 cups Bisquick® Original baking mix
1⅓ cups milk
⅓ cup orange marmalade
2 tablespoons vegetable oil
1 tablespoon sugar
1 egg
Orange butter (below)

For each waffle, brush both sides of interior of Belgian waffler with shortening. Heat both sides of waffler over medium heat until both thermometers register between B and A of "BAKE" section. (If either thermometer should indicate on the high end of "BAKE" section, cool waffler by removing from heat before pouring in batter.)

Beat remaining ingredients except Orange Butter with hand beater until smooth. Pour scant cupful batter onto center of waffler. Bake 1 minute; turn waffler. Bake until steaming stops, about 1½ minutes longer. Remove waffle carefully; keep warm. Repeat with remaining batter. Serve with Orange Butter and, if desired, maple syrup.

4 waffles

Orange Butter

½ cup (1 stick) margarine or butter, softened
1 teaspoon grated orange peel
1 tablespoon orange juice

Mix all ingredients until well blended.

FOR ELECTRIC WAFFLE IRON OR ELECTRIC BELGIAN WAFFLER: Pour scant cupful batter onto center of hot waffle iron. Bake until steaming stops. Remove carefully.

PER SERVING: Calories 665; Protein 8 g; Carbohydrate 61 g; Fat 43 g; Cholesterol 60 mg; Sodium 1180 mg

Pancakes

Pancakes are easy to personalize. Simply stir in ½ cup fresh or frozen (thawed and well drained) berries or chopped fruit— bananas, apples, peaches or pears. Serve with syrup, honey, jelly or jam to complement the fruit flavors. For crunch, you can stir in trail mix, granola or chopped nuts.

1 egg
1 cup all-purpose or whole wheat flour
¾ cup milk
1 tablespoon granulated or packed brown sugar
2 tablespoons vegetable oil
3 teaspoons baking powder
¼ teaspoon salt
Margarine, butter or shortening

Beat egg with hand beater in medium bowl until fluffy. Beat in remaining ingredients except margarine just until smooth. For thinner pancakes, stir in additional 1 to 2 tablespoons milk. Heat griddle or skillet over medium heat or to 375°. Grease griddle with margarine if necessary. (To test griddle, sprinkle with few drops water. If bubbles skitter around, heat is just right.)

For each pancake, pour scant ¼ cup batter onto hot griddle. Cook pancakes until puffed and dry around edges. Turn and cook other sides until golden brown.   **nine 4-inch pancakes**

PER SERVING: Calories 100; Protein 3 g; Carbohydrate 12 g; Fat 4 g; Cholesterol 30 mg; Sodium 215 mg

Applesauce Pancakes

1 egg
1 cup all-purpose or unbleached flour
½ cup milk
½ cup applesauce
¼ teaspoon ground cinnamon
2 tablespoons shortening, melted, or salad oil
1 tablespoon sugar
3 teaspoons baking powder
½ teaspoon salt

Beat egg with hand beater until fluffy; beat in remaining ingredients just until smooth. For thinner pancakes, stir in additional ¼ cup milk. Heat griddle or skillet over medium heat or to 375°. Grease heated griddle if necessary. (To test griddle, sprinkle with few drops water. If bubbles skitter around, heat is just right.)

Pour about 3 tablespoons batter from tip of large spoon or from pitcher onto hot griddle. Cook pancakes until puffed and dry around edges. Turn and cook other sides until golden brown.   **eleven 4-inch pancakes**

CHEESE PANCAKES: Omit applesauce, cinnamon and sugar. Stir in 1 cup shredded Swiss or American cheese (about 4 ounces).

CORNMEAL PANCAKES: Omit applesauce and cinnamon. Substitute ½ cup cornmeal for ½ cup of the flour.

PER SERVING: Calories 85; Protein 2 g; Carbohydrate 13 g; Fat 3 g; Cholesterol 20 mg; Sodium 210 mg

Buckwheat Pancakes

You can find buckwheat in specialty food stores for this simplified version of an old-time treat.

1 egg
½ cup buckwheat flour
½ cup whole wheat flour
1 cup milk
1 tablespoon sugar
2 tablespoons vegetable oil or shortening, melted
3 teaspoons baking powder
½ teaspoon salt
Whole bran or wheat germ, if desired

Beat egg with hand beater until fluffy; beat in remaining ingredients, except bran, just until smooth. Heat griddle or skillet over medium heat or to 375°. Grease heated griddle if necessary. (To test griddle, sprinkle with few drops water. If bubbles skitter around, heat is just right.)

For each pancake, pour about 3 tablespoons batter from tip of large spoon or from pitcher onto hot griddle. Cook pancakes until puffed and dry around edges. Sprinkle each pancake with 1 teaspoon whole bran. Turn and cook other sides until golden brown.

ten 4-inch pancakes

BLUEBERRY PANCAKES: Substitute 1 cup all-purpose flour for the buckwheat and whole wheat flours. Decrease milk to ¾ cup. Stir in ½ cup fresh or frozen (thawed and well drained) blueberries.

PER SERVING; Calories 95; Protein 3 g; Carbohydrate 12 g; Fat 4 g; Cholesterol 25 mg; Sodium 240 mg

Perfect Pancakes and French Toast

Heat the griddle or skillet on medium heat or set at 375° about 10 minutes before cooking pancakes or French toast. The griddle will be evenly heated, ensuring more even browning. Because pan materials and thicknesses vary, as do cooktops, adjust heat as necessary.

Fluffy Buttermilk Pancakes

3 egg yolks
1½ cups all-purpose flour
1⅔ cups buttermilk
1 tablespoon sugar
3 tablespoons butter or margarine, softened
1 teaspoon baking soda
1 teaspoon baking powder
½ teaspoon salt
3 egg whites, stiffly beaten

Beat egg yolks with hand beater. Add remaining ingredients except egg whites; beat until smooth. (For thinner pancakes, stir in 2 to 4 tablespoons additional buttermilk.) Fold in egg whites gently. Heat griddle or skillet over medium heat or to 375°. Grease heated griddle if necessary. (To test griddle, sprinkle with few drops of water. If bubbles skitter around, heat is just right.) Pour batter onto hot griddle for each pancake. Cook until puffed and dry around edges. Turn and cook other sides until golden brown. **sixteen 4-inch pancakes**

PER SERVING: Calories 95; Protein 3 g; Carbohydrate 11 g; Fat 3 g; Cholesterol 45 mg; Sodium 190 mg

Oatmeal Pancakes with Peanut Butter Spread

This easy spread of equal parts maple syrup and peanut butter is irresistible on these wholesome pancakes.

½ cup all-purpose flour
½ cup quick-cooking oats
¾ cup buttermilk
¼ cup milk
1 tablespoon sugar
2 tablespoons vegetable oil
1 teaspoon baking powder
½ teaspoon baking soda
½ teaspoon salt
1 egg
Peanut Butter Spread (below)

Beat all ingredients except Peanut Butter Spread with hand beater until smooth. (For thinner pancakes, stir in 2 to 4 tablespoons additional milk.) Heat griddle or skillet over medium heat or to 375°. Grease heated griddle if necessary. (To test griddle, sprinkle with few drops water. If bubbles skitter around, heat is just right.) Pour scant ¼ cup batter onto hot griddle for each pancake. Cook until puffed and dry around edges. Turn and cook other sides until golden brown. Serve with spread.

10 to 12 pancakes

Peanut Butter Spread

½ cup maple syrup
½ cup peanut butter

Mix syrup and peanut butter until well blended.

PER SERVING: Calories 205; Protein 6 g; Carbohydrate 23 g; Fat 10 g; Cholesterol 25 mg; Sodium 280 mg

Baked Apple and Cheese Pancake

¼ cup (½ stick) margarine or butter
1 cup all-purpose flour
1 cup milk
½ teaspoon salt
4 eggs
1 cup shredded Swiss, white Cheddar or Monterey Jack cheese (4 ounces)
½ lemon
2 medium apples or pears, thinly sliced
Powdered sugar

Heat oven to 425°. Heat margarine in rectangular pan, 13 × 9 × 2 inches, in oven until hot and bubbly. Beat flour, milk, salt and eggs until well blended. Pour into pan.

Bake until sides of pancake are puffed and deep golden brown, 20 to 25 minutes. Sprinkle with cheese. Squeeze juice from lemon over apples; arrange in center of pancake. Sprinkle with powdered sugar.

4 servings

PER SERVING: Calories 475; Protein 19 g; Carbohydrate 41 g; Fat 26 g; Cholesterol 240 mg; Sodium 560 mg

Baked Apple and Cheese Pancake

Easy Popover Pancake

3 tablespoons margarine or butter
2 eggs
½ cup milk
½ cup all-purpose flour
¼ teaspoon ground cinnamon, if desired

Heat oven to 400°. Heat margarine in 1-quart shallow round casserole or 8-inch ovenproof skillet in oven until melted. Place remaining ingredients in blender container in order listed. Cover and blend on high speed 15 seconds. Scrape sides; stir to moisten any remaining flour. Or beat ingredients with hand beater until smooth. Pour into casserole.

Bake until center is puffed and edge is golden brown, 20 to 25 minutes. Serve with fresh fruit and yogurt, if desired. **3 to 4 servings**

PER SERVING: Calories 250; Protein 8 g; Carbohydrate 18 g; Fat 16 g; Cholesterol 150 mg; Sodium 200 mg

Microwave Magic

Pancakes can be refrigerated or frozen for a quick microwave breakfast another time. Spread the pancakes with a thin layer of margarine or butter to help them reheat evenly. Tightly wrap packets of two or four or place in sealed plastic bag. Label and freeze no longer than three months or refrigerate no longer than forty-eight hours. Unwrap pancakes and place stack on plate. Cover loosely to microwave.

Pancakes	Room Temperature	Frozen
2	1 minute to 1½ minutes	2 to 3 minutes
4	2 to 3 minutes	3 to 4 minutes

Crepes

1½ cups all-purpose flour
1 tablespoon sugar
½ teaspoon baking powder
½ teaspoon salt
2 cups milk
2 tablespoons margarine or butter, melted
½ teaspoon vanilla
2 eggs

Mix flour, sugar, baking powder and salt in 1½-quart bowl. Stir in remaining ingredients. Beat with hand beater until smooth. Lightly butter 6- to 8-inch skillet; heat over medium heat until bubbly. For each crepe, pour scant ¼ cup of the batter into skillet; *immediately* rotate skillet until thin film covers bottom.

Cook until light brown. Run wide spatula around edge to loosen; turn and cook other side until light brown. Stack crepes, placing waxed paper between each. Keep covered.

If desired, thinly spread applesauce, sweetened strawberries, currant jelly or raspberry jam on warm crepes; roll up. (Be sure to fill crepes so the more attractive side is on the outside.) Sprinkle with powdered sugar if desired.

12 crepes

NOTE: Crepes can be frozen up to 3 months. To freeze, cool; keep crepes covered to prevent them from drying out. Make 2 stacks of 6 crepes each, with waxed paper between crepes. Wrap each stack in aluminum foil, label and freeze.

PER SERVING: Calories 110; Protein 4 g; Carbohydrate 15 g; Fat 4 g; Cholesterol 40 mg; Sodium 160 mg

Raspberry Crepes

Crepes (page 44)
1 package (3½ ounces) vanilla instant
   pudding and pie filling
2 cups half-and-half
½ teaspoon almond extract
2 tablespoons cornstarch
2 packages (10 ounces each) frozen raspberries, thawed
Sliced almonds

Prepare Crepes. Prepare pudding and pie filling as directed on package for pudding—except substitute half-and-half for the milk and beat in almond extract; refrigerate until chilled.

Place cornstarch in 1½-quart saucepan; gradually stir in raspberries. Cook over medium heat, stirring constantly, until mixture thickens and boils. Boil and stir 1 minute; cool. Spoon generous 2 tablespoons pudding mixture onto each crepe; roll up. Place 2 crepes, seam sides down, on each dessert plate. Top with raspberry mixture and sprinkle with slices almonds.

6 servings

PER SERVING: Calories 525; Protein 12 g; Carbohydrate 77 g; Fat 19 g; Cholesterol 110 mg; Sodium 590 mg

Cherry Blintzes

Crepes (page 44)
1 cup dry cottage cheese
½ cup sour cream
2 tablespoons sugar
1 teaspoon vanilla
½ teaspoon grated lemon peel
¼ cup (½ stick) margarine or butter
1 cup sour cream
1 can (21 ounces) cherry pie filling

Prepare Crepes as directed—except brown only one side. Cool, keeping crepes covered to prevent them from drying out.

Mix cottage cheese, ½ cup sour cream, the sugar, vanilla and lemon peel. Spoon about 1½ tablespoons of the cheese mixture onto browned side of each crepe. Fold sides of crepe up over filling, overlapping edges; roll up.

Heat margarine in 12-inch skillet over medium heat until bubbly. Place blintzes, seam sides down, in skillet. Cook, turning once, until golden brown. Top each with rounded tablespoon sour cream and about 3 tablespoons pie filling.

6 servings

PER SERVING: Calories 695; Protein 14 g; Carbohydrate 101 g; Fat 26 g; Cholesterol 120 mg; Sodium 470 mg

Tuna Crepe Cups

An unusual, and unusually tasty, twist on crepes.

Crepes (below)
¼ cup finely chopped onion
¼ cup finely chopped green bell pepper
1 can (6½ ounces) tuna in water, drained
4 eggs
1 cup milk
½ teaspoon salt
½ teaspoon dry mustard
⅛ teaspoon ground red pepper (cayenne)
¼ cup grated Parmesan cheese

Prepare Crepes. Heat oven to 350°. Carefully fit 1 crepe in each of 12 greased muffin cups, 2½ × 1¼ inches. Divide onion, bell pepper and tuna among crepe-lined cups. Beat eggs, milk, salt, mustard and red pepper until smooth. Pour about 3 tablespoons egg mixture into each cup. Sprinkle with cheese. Bake until knife inserted in center comes out clean, 20 to 25 minutes. (If edges of crepes begin to brown before eggs are set, cover with aluminum foil.) Let stand 5 minutes before serving. **6 servings**

Crepes

1 cup all-purpose flour
¼ teaspoon baking powder
¼ teaspoon salt
1¼ cups milk
1 egg
1 tablespoon margarine or butter, melted

Mix flour, baking powder and salt. Stir in remaining ingredients. Beat with hand beater until smooth. Lightly butter 6-inch skillet; heat over medium heat until bubbly. For each crepe, pour scant ¼ cup of the batter into skillet; immediately rotate skillet until thin film of batter covers bottom. Cook until light brown. Run wide spatula around edge to loosen; turn and cook other side until light brown. Stack crepes, placing waxed paper between each. Keep crepes covered to prevent them from drying out.

SALMON CREPE CUPS: Substitute 1 can (7¾ ounces) salmon, drained, cleaned and flaked, for the tuna.

PER SERVING: Calories 225; Protein 20 g; Carbohydrate 24 g; Fat 9 g; Cholesterol 190 mg; Sodium 1220 mg

French Toast

To test griddle, sprinkle with a few drops of water. If bubbles skitter around, heat is just right.

2 eggs, beaten
½ cup milk
¼ teaspoon salt
Margarine or butter
6 slices day-old bread

Beat eggs, milk and salt until blended. Grease heated griddle with thin layer of margarine. Dip bread into egg mixture. Cook bread on griddle until golden brown. **6 slices**

PER SERVING: Calories 105; Protein 5 g; Carbohydrate 14 g; Fat 3 g; Cholesterol 70 mg; Sodium 250 mg

French Toast

French Toast for a Crowd

You'll find this recipe handy when you want to serve a large group of people.

½ cup all-purpose flour
1½ cups milk
1 tablespoon sugar
½ teaspoon vanilla
¼ teaspoon salt
6 eggs
Margarine, butter or shortening
18 slices French bread, each 1 inch thick

Beat flour, milk, sugar, vanilla, salt and eggs with hand beater until smooth. Heat griddle or skillet over medium heat or to 375°. Grease griddle with margarine if necessary. (To test griddle, sprinkle with few drops water. If bubbles skitter around, heat is just right.)

Dip bread into egg mixture. Cook about 4 minutes on each side or until golden brown.

18 slices

CUSTARDY OVERNIGHT FRENCH TOAST: Prepare as directed—except arrange bread slices just to fit in single layer in glass baking dish. Pour egg mixture over bread slices. Turn to coat both sides. Cover and refrigerate overnight. Cook as directed—except increase cooking time to 6 to 8 minutes on each side.

PER SERVING: Calories 130; Protein 5 g; Carbohydrate 18 g; Fat 4 g; Cholesterol 95 mg; Sodium 220 mg

New Orleans French Toast

Serve this French-inspired treat with the maple syrup suggested, or top with fresh orange sections tossed with sugar and orange liqueur.

⅔ cup milk
1 tablespoon powdered sugar
¼ teaspoon salt
1 teaspoon grated orange peel
3 eggs
2 tablespoons margarine or butter
8 slices day-old bread

Beat all ingredients except margarine and bread until smooth. Heat 1 tablespoon of the margarine in 10-inch skillet over medium heat until melted. Dip several bread slices into egg mixture (stir egg mixture each time before dipping bread). Cook about 2 minutes on each side or until golden brown. Repeat with remaining bread slices, adding remaining margarine as needed. Sprinkle with powdered sugar and serve with maple syrup if desired. **4 servings**

PER SERVING: Calories 270; Protein 10 g; Carbohydrate 30 g; Fat 12 g; Cholesterol 180 mg; Sodium 490 mg

Surprise French Toast

Use jams, jellies or peanut butter as a "surprise" in your French toast, along with the cream cheese in the recipe.

  1 package (3 ounces) cream cheese
  16 slices (½ inch thick) French bread
  1 cup milk
  4 eggs
  2 tablespoons margarine or butter
  Powdered sugar
  Syrup

Spread 1 tablespoon cream cheese on each of 8 slices bread; top with second slice bread. Whisk together milk and eggs in large bowl.

Heat griddle or large skillet over medium heat or to 350°; melt margarine. Dip sandwiches in egg mixture; carefully place on griddle. Cook about 8 minutes on each side until golden brown. Sprinkle with powdered sugar; serve with syrup. **4 servings**

PER SERVING: Calories 505; Protein 19 g; Carbohydrate 62 g; Fat 20 g; Cholesterol 240 mg; Sodium 810 mg

Oven French Toast

A wonderful recipe for a busy morning.

  3 tablespoons margarine or butter, melted
  ⅓ cup orange juice
  2 tablespoons honey
  3 eggs
  8 slices French bread, each 1 inch thick

Pour margarine into jelly roll pan, 15½ × 10½ × 1 inch. Beat orange juice, honey and eggs with hand beater until foamy. Dip bread into egg mixture; place in pan. Drizzle any remaining egg mixture over bread. Cover and refrigerate no longer than 24 hours.

Heat oven to 450°. Bake uncovered until bottoms are golden brown, about 10 minutes; turn bread. Bake until bottoms are golden brown, 6 to 8 minutes longer. **4 servings**

PER SERVING: Calories 190; Protein 5 g; Carbohydrate 16 g; Fat 12 g; Cholesterol 160 mg; Sodium 200 mg

Blueberry-Streusel Muffins

3

Delectable Baked Goods

Blueberry-Streusel Muffins

Streusel Topping (right)
1 cup milk
⅓ cup vegetable oil
½ teaspoon vanilla
1 egg
2 cups all-purpose or whole wheat flour
⅓ cup sugar
3 teaspoons baking powder
½ teaspoon salt
1 cup fresh or frozen (thawed and well drained) blueberries

Heat oven to 400°. Grease bottoms only of 12 medium muffin cups, 2½ × 1¼ inches, or line with paper baking cups. Prepare Streusel Topping; reserve.

Beat milk, oil, vanilla and egg in large bowl. Stir in flour, sugar, baking powder and salt just until flour is moistened. Fold in blueberries. Divide batter evenly among muffin cups (cups will be about ¾ full). Sprinkle each with about 2 teaspoons Streusel Topping. Bake 22 to 24 minutes

or until golden brown. Immediately remove from pan. **12 muffins**

Streusel Topping

2 tablespoons firm margarine or butter
¼ cup all-purpose flour
2 tablespoons packed brown sugar
¼ teaspoon ground cinnamon

Cut margarine into remaining ingredients in small bowl until crumbly.

JUMBO BLUEBERRY-STREUSEL MUFFINS: Heat oven to 375°. Grease bottoms only of 4 jumbo muffin cups, 3½ × 1¾ inches. Divide batter and Streusel Topping evenly among muffin cups (cups will be almost full). Bake about 25 minutes, until toothpick inserted in center comes out clean. Let stand 5 minutes before removing from pan.

4 jumbo muffins

PER SERVING: Calories 210; Protein 3 g; Carbohydrate 29 g; Fat 9 g; Cholesterol 20 mg; Sodium 220 mg

Applesauce-Graham Muffins

If the raisins stick together, toss them with a little flour. You'll have a more even distribution of raisins throughout the muffin batter.

¾ cup chunky applesauce
⅓ cup packed brown sugar
⅓ cup margarine or butter, melted
1 egg
1 cup all-purpose flour
⅔ cup graham cracker crumbs (about nine 2½-inch squares)
2 teaspoons baking powder
1 teaspoon baking soda
1 teaspoon ground cinnamon
1 cup raisins

Heat oven to 400°. Grease bottoms only of 12 medium muffin cups, 2½ × 1¼ inches, or line with paper baking cups. Beat applesauce, brown sugar, margarine and egg in large bowl. Stir in remaining ingredients except raisins just until flour is moistened. Fold in raisins. Divide batter evenly among muffin cups (cups will be almost full). Bake 18 to 20 minutes or until golden brown. Immediately remove from pan.

12 muffins

MINI APPLESAUCE-GRAHAM MUFFINS: Grease bottoms only of 24 small muffin cups, 1¾ × 1 inch. Divide batter evenly among muffins cups (cups will be very full). Bake 11 to 13 minutes or until golden brown. **24 mini muffins**

PER SERVING: Calories 185; Protein 2 g; Carbohydrate 31 g; Fat 6 g; Cholesterol 20 mg; Sodium 230 mg

Tropical Banana Muffins

Chopping candied pineapple will be easier if you dip the knife into water before you begin.

1 cup mashed ripe bananas (about 2 medium)
½ cup packed brown sugar
⅓ cup milk
¼ cup vegetable oil
1 egg
2 cups all-purpose flour
2½ teaspoons baking powder
½ teaspoon salt
½ cup chopped macadamia nuts or pecans
¼ cup flaked coconut
¼ cup chopped candied pineapple

Heat oven to 400°. Grease bottoms only of 12 medium muffin cups, 2½ × 1¼ inches, or line with paper baking cups. Beat bananas, brown sugar, milk, oil and egg in large bowl. Stir in flour, baking powder and salt just until flour is moistened. Fold in macadamia nuts, coconut and pineapple. Divide batter evenly among muffin cups (cups will be very full). Bake 18 to 20 minutes or until golden brown. Immediately remove from pan. **12 muffins**

PER SERVING: Calories 230; Protein 3 g; Carbohydrate 34 g; Fat 9 g; Cholesterol 20 mg; Sodium 210 mg

Spiced Honey-Lemon Muffins

Some of the warm glaze will drip off the warm muffins, so place muffins on a serving plate, cookie sheet or waxed paper for easier cleanup.

¾ **cup milk**
⅓ **cup vegetable oil**
¼ **cup honey**
2 **teaspoons grated lemon peel**
1 **egg**
2 **cups all-purpose flour**
2½ **teaspoons baking powder**
½ **teaspoon salt**
½ **teaspoon ground cinnamon**
¼ **teaspoon ground allspice**
Honey-Lemon Glaze (below)

Heat oven to 400°. Grease bottoms only of 8 medium muffin cups, 2½ × 1¼ inches, or line with paper baking cups. Beat milk, oil, honey, lemon peel and egg in large bowl. Stir in remaining ingredients except Honey-Lemon Glaze just until flour is moistened. Divide batter evenly among muffin cups (cups will be about ¾ full). Bake 20 to 22 minutes or until golden brown. Immediately remove from pan. Brush Honey-Lemon Glaze over warm muffins.

8 muffins

Honey-Lemon Glaze

2 **tablespoons honey**
¼ **teaspoon grated lemon peel**
2 **teaspoons lemon juice**

Mix all ingredients until well blended.

BAKERY-STYLE SPICED HONEY-LEMON MUFFINS: Grease bottoms only of 6 medium muffin cups, 2½ × 1¼ inches, or line with paper baking cups. Divide batter evenly among muffin cups (cups will be very full). Bake 22 to 24 minutes or until golden brown. **6 muffins**

PER SERVING: Calories 260; Protein 4 g; Carbohydrate 38 g; Fat 10 g; Cholesterol 30 mg; Sodium 270 mg

Baking Muffins

• Place the oven rack in the center of the oven for the best circulation of heat.

• Divide batter evenly among muffin cups, using a large spoon or ice-cream scoop. Wipe off any batter that spills onto the edge of the pan to avoid burning. Fill empty cups in the muffin pan half full of water to ensure even baking.

• Bake muffins for the minimum time specified in the recipe, then check for doneness. If necessary, bake a minute or two longer, then check them again.

• When muffins are done, immediately remove them from the muffin pan. Occasionally, a recipe will specify that muffins be left in the pan for a few minutes before removing; this allows fragile muffins to set up.

Brown Sugar Muffins

1 cup quick-cooking oats
½ cup milk
¾ cup packed brown sugar
¼ cup (½ stick) margarine or butter, melted
1 egg
1 cup all-purpose flour
½ cup chopped walnuts
2 teaspoons baking powder

Heat oven to 400°. Grease 12 medium muffin cups, 2½ × 1¼ inches. Mix oats, milk and brown sugar in large bowl; let stand 5 minutes. Add margarine and egg; blend well. Stir in remaining ingredients just until moistened. Fill muffin cups two-thirds full. Bake 15 to 20 minutes or until wooden pick inserted in center comes out clean. **12 muffins**

PER SERVING: Calories 195; Protein 3 g; Carbohydrate 28 g; Fat 8 g; Cholesterol 20 mg; Sodium 125 mg

Reheating Muffins

- Muffins are best served warm. If they become too cool, heat uncovered in the microwave on medium (50%) just until warm—one muffin for 15 to 30 seconds, two muffins for 25 to 40 seconds, three muffins for 35 to 60 seconds and four muffins for 45 seconds to 1 minute 15 seconds.

- Or to reheat in a conventional oven, wrap muffins in aluminum foil and heat in a 400° oven about 5 minutes or until warm.

Hawaiian Chocolate Muffins

Muffins take a tropical turn with the addition of pineapple and macadamia nuts. These generous muffins are great served with fresh fruit and ham, and make any breakfast special.

⅓ cup vegetable oil
2 eggs
1 can (8¼ ounces) crushed pineapple, undrained
1¾ cups all-purpose flour
¼ cup cocoa
⅓ cup sugar
3 teaspoons baking powder
½ cup chopped macadamia nuts
Orange glaze (below), if desired

Heat oven to 400°. Grease bottoms only of 12 medium muffin cups, 2½ × 1¼ inches, or line with paper baking cups. Beat oil, eggs and pineapple. Stir in remaining ingredients except Orange Glaze just until flour is moistened. Divide batter evenly among muffin cups. Bake 20 to 25 minutes or until toothpick inserted in center comes out clean. Immediately remove from pan to wire rack. Serve warm with warm Orange Glaze or serve cool. **12 muffins**

Orange Glaze

⅓ cup margarine or butter
2 cups powdered sugar
½ teaspoon grated orange peel
2 to 4 tablespoons orange juice

Heat margarine in saucepan until melted. Stir in powdered sugar and orange peel. Stir in orange juice, 1 tablespoon at a time, until smooth and of drizzling consistency.

about 2 cups glaze

PER SERVING: Calories 210; Protein 3 g; Carbohydrate 25 g; Fat 11 g; Cholesterol 35 mg; Sodium 130 mg

Hawaiian Chocolate Muffins

Orange-Rye Muffins

1¼ cups all-purpose flour
¾ cup rye flour
2 tablespoons sugar
3 teaspoons baking powder
¼ teaspoon salt
½ cup orange juice
½ cup vegetable oil
1 tablespoon grated orange peel
2 eggs
1 tablespoon sugar

Heat oven to 400°. Grease 12 medium muffin cups, 2½ × 1¼ inches, or line with paper baking cups. Mix flours, 2 tablespoons sugar, baking powder and salt in large bowl. Stir in remaining ingredients except 1 tablespoon sugar, just until moistened. Fill muffin cups two-thirds full. Sprinkle batter with 1 tablespoon sugar. Bake 12 to 18 minutes until muffins are golden brown. Remove from pan; cool. **12 muffins**

PER SERVING: Calories 180; Protein 3 g; Carbohydrate 20 g; Fat 10 g; Cholesterol 35 mg; Sodium 150 mg

Vegetable-Cornmeal Muffins

1¼ cups yellow cornmeal
¾ cup all-purpose flour
¼ cup shortening
1½ cups buttermilk
2 teaspoons baking powder
1 teaspoon sugar
1 teaspoon salt
½ teaspoon baking soda
2 eggs
1 cup shredded zucchini, drained
½ cup chopped red bell pepper
2 tablespoons chopped jalapeño or serrano chiles

Heat oven to 450°. Grease 16 medium muffin cups, 2½ × 1¼ inches, or line muffin cups with paper baking cups. Mix all ingredients except zucchini, bell pepper and chiles; beat vigorously 30 seconds. Stir in remaining ingredients. Fill muffin cups about seven-eighths full. Bake until light golden brown, 20 to 25 minutes. Remove from pan immediately. **16 muffins**

PER SERVING: Calories 110; Protein 3 g; Carbohydrate 15 g; Fat 4 g; Cholesterol 30 mg; Sodium 250 mg

Wine-and-Cheese Muffins

Delicious served with wine and light foods such as fish and salads that don't hide the delicate flavors.

2 cups Bisquick® Original baking mix
⅔ cup white wine or apple juice
2 tablespoons vegetable oil
1 egg
1 cup shredded Swiss, Gruyère or Cheddar cheese (4 ounces)
2 teaspoons chopped fresh or freeze-dried chives

Heat oven to 400°. Line 12 medium muffin cups, 2½ × 1¼ inches, with paper baking cups, or grease entire cups generously. Mix baking mix, wine, oil and egg with fork. Beat vigorously 30 strokes. Stir in remaining ingredients. Divide batter evenly among cups. Bake about 20 minutes or until golden brown.   **12 muffins**

TO MICROWAVE: Prepare batter as directed. Spoon batter into 6 paper baking cups in microwavable muffin ring, filling each about three-fourths full. Microwave uncovered on high 2 to 3 minutes, rotating ring ¼ turn every minute, until wooden pick inserted in center comes out clean (edges of muffins may appear slightly moist). Cool 1 minute; remove from ring. Repeat with remaining batter.

PER SERVING: Calories 150; Protein 4 g; Carbohydrate 14 g; Fat 9 g; Cholesterol 35 mg; Sodium 300 mg

French Breakfast Puffs

⅓ cup shortening
½ cup sugar
1 egg
1½ cups all-purpose flour
1½ teaspoons baking powder
½ teaspoon salt
¼ teaspoon ground nutmeg
½ cup milk
½ cup sugar
1 teaspoon ground cinnamon
½ cup (1 stick) margarine or butter, melted

Heat oven to 350°. Grease 15 medium muffin cups, 2½ × 1¼ inches. Mix shortening, ½ cup sugar and the egg thoroughly. Mix flour, baking powder, salt and nutmeg; stir into egg mixture alternately with milk. Fill muffin cups two-thirds full. Bake 20 to 25 minutes or until golden brown. Mix ½ cup sugar and the cinnamon. Roll hot muffins immediately in melted margarine, then in sugar-cinnamon mixture. Serve hot.

15 puffs

PER SERVING: Calories 205; Protein 2 g; Carbohydrate 24 g; Fat 11 g; Cholesterol 30 mg; Sodium 160 mg

Buttermilk Drop Doughnuts

These little morsels are quick to make, and melt-in-your-mouth good!

Vegetable oil
2 cups all-purpose flour
¼ cup sugar
1 teaspoon salt
1 teaspoon baking powder
1 teaspoon ground nutmeg
½ teaspoon baking soda
¼ cup vegetable oil
¾ cup buttermilk
1 egg
Sugar or cinnamon sugar

Heat oil (2 to 3 inches) in Dutch oven to 375°. Mix flour, ¼ cup sugar, the salt, baking powder, nutmeg and baking soda in large bowl. Add oil, buttermilk and egg; beat with fork until smooth. Drop batter by teaspoonfuls (do not make too large or they will not cook through) into hot oil. Fry about 3 minutes or until golden brown on both sides; drain on paper towels. Immediately roll in sugar. **about 42 doughnuts**

PER SERVING: Calories 60; Protein 1 g; Carbohydrate 7 g; Fat 3 g; Cholesterol 5 mg; Sodium 175 mg

Glazed Chocolate Oven Doughnuts

2⅓ cups Bisquick® Original baking mix
¼ cup sugar
½ cup milk
3 tablespoons cocoa
1 teaspoon vanilla
Chocolate Glaze (below)

Heat oven to 425°. Mix all ingredients except Chocolate Glaze until dough forms. Turn dough onto surface dusted with baking mix; gently roll in baking mix to coat. Knead lightly 10 times. Roll dough ½ inch thick. Cut with 2½-inch doughnut cutter. Place about 2 inches apart on ungreased cookie sheet.

Bake about 8 minutes or until set; remove from cookie sheet. Cool slightly on wire rack. Spread with Chocolate Glaze. Sprinkle with chopped nuts, coconut or multicolored candy shot if desired. **about 9 doughnuts**

Chocolate Glaze

½ cup semisweet chocolate chips
1 tablespoon shortening

Heat ingredients in heavy 1-quart saucepan over low heat, stirring occasionally, until melted.

PER SERVING: Calories 230; Protein 3 g; Carbohydrate 34 g; Fat 9 g; Cholesterol 5 mg; Sodium 460 mg

Glazed Chocolate Oven Doughnuts and Cinnamon Crispies

Cinnamon Crispies

½ cup (1 stick) margarine or butter
2 cups all-purpose flour
¼ cup sugar
⅔ cup milk
1 teaspoon baking powder
1 teaspoon salt
⅓ cup sugar
2 teaspoons ground cinnamon
Sugar

Heat oven to 425°. Grease 2 cookie sheets. Heat margarine until melted; reserve 2 tablespoons. Mix remaining margarine, the flour, ¼ cup sugar, the milk, baking powder and salt in large bowl until dough forms. Turn dough onto lightly floured surface; gently roll in flour to coat. Knead lightly 10 times.

Divide dough into halves. Roll or pat one half of dough into rectangle, 9 × 5 inches. Brush with half of reserved melted margarine. Mix ⅓ cup sugar and the cinnamon; sprinkle half over rectangle. Roll up tightly, beginning at 5-inch side. Pinch edge of dough into roll to seal. Cut roll into 4 equal pieces with sharp knife. Place cut sides up on cookie sheets; pat each into 6-inch circle. Sprinkle with sugar.

Bake 8 to 10 minutes or until edges are golden brown. Immediately remove from cookie sheets with metal spatula. Cool on wire rack. Repeat with remaining dough, melted margarine and cinnamon-sugar mixture.   **8 crispies**

PER SERVING: Calories 290; Protein 4 g; Carbohydrate 42 g; Fat 12 g; Cholesterol 5 mg; Sodium 460 mg

Baking Powder Biscuits

Baking powder biscuits are a breakfast staple—they make just about any meal special.

½ cup shortening
2 cups all-purpose flour
1 tablespoon sugar
3 teaspoons baking powder
1 teaspoon salt
About ¾ cup milk

Heat oven to 450°. Cut shortening into flour, sugar, baking powder and salt with pastry blender in large bowl until mixture resembles fine crumbs. Stir in just enough milk so dough leaves side of bowl and forms a ball.

Turn dough onto lightly floured surface; gently roll in flour to coat. Knead lightly 10 times. Roll or pat ½ inch thick. Cut with floured 2½-inch biscuit cutter. Place about 1 inch apart on ungreased cookie sheet. Bake 10 to 12 minutes or until golden brown. Immediately remove from cookie sheet. Serve hot.

about 10 biscuits

PER SERVING: Calories 195; Protein 3 g; Carbohydrate 21 g; Fat 11 g; Cholesterol 5 mg; Sodium 340 mg

Buttermilk Biscuits

If you don't have buttermilk on hand, mix 2¼ teaspoons vinegar and enough milk to make ¾ cup. Let the mixture stand a few minutes until slightly thickened.

½ **cup shortening**
2 **cups all-purpose flour**
1 **tablespoon sugar**
2 **teaspoons baking powder**
1 **teaspoon salt**
¼ **teaspoon baking soda**
About ¾ cup buttermilk

Heat oven to 450°. Cut shortening into flour, sugar, baking powder, salt and baking soda with pastry blender in large bowl until mixture resembles fine crumbs. Stir in just enough buttermilk so dough leaves side of bowl and forms a ball.

Turn dough onto lightly floured surface; gently roll in flour to coat. Knead lightly 10 times. Roll or pat ½ inch thick. Cut with floured 2½-inch biscuit cutter. Place about 1 inch apart on ungreased cookie sheet. Bake 10 to 12 minutes or until golden brown. Immediately remove from cookie sheet. Serve hot.

about 10 biscuits

PER SERVING: Calories 195; Protein 3 g; Carbohydrate 21 g; Fat 11 g; Cholesterol 1 mg; Sodium 330 mg

Biscuit Baking Tips

• Place oven rack in center position for the best circulation of heat.

• Place unbaked biscuits on an ungreased shiny cookie sheet. A dark, nonstick or dull cookie sheet can result in biscuits with dark brown bottoms. If you have a dark cookie sheet, reduce the oven temperature by 25°.

• For biscuits with soft sides, place biscuits with sides touching on an ungreased shiny pan.

• Bake until golden brown. Immediately remove from cookie sheet; serve hot.

Bulgur Biscuits

Bulgur Biscuits

¼ cup shortening
1 cup all-purpose flour
1 cup whole wheat flour
3 teaspoons baking powder
½ teaspoon salt
½ cup cooked bulgur or brown rice
About ⅔ cup skim milk

Heat oven to 450°. Cut shortening into flours, baking powder and salt with pastry blender in large bowl until mixture resembles fine crumbs. Stir in bulgur. Stir in just enough milk so dough leaves side of bowl and forms a ball.

Turn dough onto lightly floured surface; gently roll in flour to coat. Knead lightly 10 times. Roll or pat ½ inch thick. Cut with floured 2½-inch biscuit cutter. Place about 1 inch apart on ungreased cookie sheet. Bake 12 to 14 minutes or until golden brown. Immediately remove from cookie sheet. Serve hot.

about 10 biscuits

PER SERVING: Calories 150; Protein 3 g; Carbohydrate 21 g; Fat 6 g; Cholesterol 0 mg; Sodium 280 mg

Orange-Currant Scones

½ cup currants
⅓ cup margarine or butter
1¾ cups all-purpose flour
3 tablespoons sugar
2½ teaspoons baking powder
¼ teaspoon salt
1 tablespoon grated orange peel
1 egg, beaten
4 to 6 tablespoons half-and-half
1 egg white, beaten

Heat oven to 400°. Soak currants in warm water for 10 minutes to soften; drain. Cut margarine into flour, sugar, baking powder and salt with pastry blender until mixture resembles fine crumbs. Stir in orange peel, egg, currants and just enough half-and-half until dough leaves side of bowl.

Turn dough onto lightly floured surface. Knead lightly 10 times. Divide dough into 2 parts. Roll or pat into two 6-inch circles about ½ inch thick. Place on ungreased cookie sheet; brush with beaten egg white. Bake 10 to 12 minutes or until golden brown. Immediately remove from cookie sheet. Cut into wedges to serve.

about 20 scones

PER SERVING: Calories 95; Protein 2 g; Carbohydrate 13 g; Fat 4 g; Cholesterol 10 mg; Sodium 120 mg

Make-ahead Raisin Brioche

1 package active dry yeast
3 tablespoons warm water
2 teaspoons sugar
3½ cups all-purpose flour
½ cup sugar
1 teaspoon ground cinnamon
½ teaspoon salt
¾ cup (1½ sticks) cold margarine or butter, cut up
⅓ cup milk
3 eggs
1½ cups golden raisins
1 egg white, beaten

Mix yeast, water and 2 teaspoons sugar in small bowl; set aside. Place flour, ½ cup sugar, the cinnamon and salt in food processor fitted with steel blade; cover and process until mixed. Add margarine; process until well blended.

Whisk milk and eggs into yeast mixture; slowly add to flour mixture and process until well blended. Stir in raisins. (Dough will be sticky.)

Turn dough out onto well-floured surface. Knead 1 minute until dough is smooth, adding more flour if necessary. Place in large greased bowl; cover tightly. Let dough rise in warm place 40 minutes.

Grease 12 large muffin cups, 3½ × 1½ inches. Punch dough down. Using about ¼ cup dough each, make 12 balls; place in muffin cups. Using about 1 tablespoon dough each, make 12 smaller balls; place on top of each large ball. Cover and refrigerate overnight.

Remove rolls from refrigerator. Let rise in warm place 40 to 45 minutes or until almost double in size. Heat oven to 350°. Uncover; brush rolls with beaten egg white. Bake 22 to 26 minutes until golden brown. **12 brioches**

PER SERVING: Calories 355; Protein 6 g; Carbohydrate 53 g; Fat 13 g; Cholesterol 50 mg; Sodium 250 mg

Caramel Sticky Rolls

Fragrant, tender Caramel Sticky Rolls will entice even the sleepiest person out of bed.

3½ to 4 cups all-purpose flour
⅓ cup granulated sugar
1 teaspoon salt
2 packages quick-acting or regular active dry yeast
1 cup very warm milk (120° to 130°)
⅓ cup margarine or butter, softened
1 egg
1 cup packed brown sugar
½ cup (1 stick) margarine or butter
¼ cup dark corn syrup
¾ cup pecan halves
2 tablespoons margarine or butter, softened
½ cup chopped pecans
2 tablespoons granulated sugar
2 tablespoons packed brown sugar
1 teaspoon ground cinnamon

Mix 2 cups of the flour, ⅓ cup granulated sugar, the salt and yeast in large bowl. Add warm milk, ⅓ cup margarine and the egg. Beat on low speed 1 minute, scraping bowl frequently. Beat on medium speed 1 minute, scraping bowl frequently. Stir in enough remaining flour to make dough easy to handle.

Turn dough onto lightly floured surface. Knead about 5 minutes or until smooth and elastic. Place in greased bowl and turn greased side up. Cover and let rise in warm place about 1½ hours or until double. (Dough is ready if indentation remains when touched.)

Heat 1 cup brown sugar and ½ cup margarine to boiling, stirring constantly; remove from heat. Stir in corn syrup. Pour into ungreased rectangular pan, 13 × 9 × 2 inches. Sprinkle with pecan halves.

Punch down dough. Flatten with hands or rolling pin into rectangle, 15 × 10 inches, on lightly floured surface. Spread with 2 tablespoons margarine. Mix chopped pecans, 2 tablespoons granulated sugar, 2 tablespoons brown sugar and the cinnamon. Sprinkle evenly over margarine. Roll up tightly, beginning at 15-inch side. Pinch edge of dough into roll to seal. Stretch and shape until even. Cut roll into fifteen 1-inch slices. Place slightly apart in pan. Let rise in warm place about 30 minutes or until double.

Heat oven to 350°. Bake 30 to 35 minutes or until golden brown. Immediately invert on heatproof tray or serving plate. Let stand 1 minute so caramel will drizzle down; remove pan.

15 rolls

JUMBO CARAMEL STICKY ROLLS: Prepare dough as directed—except roll dough, beginning at 10-inch side. Cut into eight 1¼-inch slices.

8 rolls

OVERNIGHT CARAMEL STICKY ROLLS: Prepare dough as directed—except do not let dough rise after placing rolls in pan. Wrap pan tightly with heavy-duty aluminum foil. Refrigerate at least 12 hours but no longer than 48 hours. Bake as directed.

PER SERVING: Calories 385; Protein 5 g; Carbohydrate 53 g; Fat 18 g; Cholesterol 20 mg; Sodium 285 mg

Blueberry Buckle Coffee Cake

A classic "buckle" is made by covering a layer of fruit with a cake batter and sweet crumbs. This coffee cake, made buckle fashion, will buckle and crack as it bakes.

2 cups all-purpose flour
¾ cup sugar
2½ teaspoons baking powder
¾ teaspoon salt
¼ cup shortening
¾ cup milk
1 egg
2 cups fresh or frozen (thawed and drained) blueberries
Crumb topping (right)
Glaze (right)

Heat oven to 375°. Grease square pan, 9 × 9 × 2 inches, or round pan, 9 × 1½ inches. Blend flour, sugar, baking powder, salt, shortening, milk and egg; beat 30 seconds. Carefully stir in blueberries. Spread batter in pan; sprinkle with Crumb Topping. Bake 45 to 50 minutes or until wooden pick inserted in center comes out clean. Drizzle with Glaze. Serve warm.

9 servings

Crumb Topping

½ cup sugar
⅓ cup all-purpose flour
½ teaspoon ground cinnamon
¼ cup (½ stick) margarine or butter, softened

Mix all ingredients until crumbly.

Glaze

½ cup powdered sugar
¼ teaspoon vanilla
1½ to 2 teaspoons hot water

Mix all ingredients until of drizzling consistency.

PER SERVING: Calories 390; Protein 5 g; Carbohydrate 65 g; Fat 12 g; Cholesterol 40 mg; Sodium 340 mg

Blueberry Buckle Coffee Cake

Cherry-Almond Coffee Cake

If you use a tube pan with this recipe, you'll need to use about ½ cup finely chopped almonds to coat the pan.

⅓ cup finely chopped almonds
1 cup sugar
½ cup (1 stick) margarine or butter, softened
½ cup milk
½ teaspoon almond extract
1 container (15 ounces) ricotta cheese
2 eggs
2½ cups all-purpose flour
1 cup dried cherries or prunes, chopped
1 cup chopped almonds, toasted if desired
3 teaspoons baking powder
½ teaspoon salt

Heat oven to 350°. Grease 12-cup bundt cake pan or tube pan, 10 × 4 inches. Coat pan with ⅓ cup finely chopped almonds. Beat sugar, margarine, milk, almond extract, cheese and eggs in large bowl on low speed until blended. Beat on medium speed 2 minutes, scraping bowl occasionally. Beat in remaining ingredients (batter will be very thick). Spread in pan.

Bake 55 to 65 minutes or until toothpick inserted near center comes out clean. Cool 20 minutes. Remove from pan; place on wire rack. Sprinkle with powdered sugar if desired. Serve warm or let stand until cool. **16 servings**

PER SERVING: Calories 320; Protein 8 g; Carbohydrate 38 g; Fat 15 g; Cholesterol 35 mg; Sodium 250 mg

Poppy Seed–Walnut Coffee Cake

Poppy Seed Filling (below)
2 cups all-purpose flour
¾ cup packed brown sugar
⅓ cup margarine or butter, softened
1 cup milk
2½ teaspoons baking powder
½ teaspoon salt
½ teaspoon ground cinnamon
¼ teaspoon ground nutmeg
1 egg
½ cup chopped walnuts
¼ cup chopped walnuts

Heat oven to 350°. Grease square pan, 9 × 9 × 2 inches. Prepare Poppy Seed Filling; reserve. Beat remaining ingredients except walnuts in large bowl on low speed until blended. Beat on medium speed 1 minute, scraping bowl occasionally. Stir in ½ cup walnuts. Spread half of the batter in pan. Spoon Poppy Seed Filling by small spoonfuls onto batter; carefully spread over batter. Spoon remaining batter over Poppy Seed Filling; carefully spread to cover Poppy Seed Filling. Sprinkle with ¼ cup walnuts. Bake 40 to 45 minutes or until toothpick inserted in center comes out clean. Serve warm or let stand until cool. Sprinkle with powdered sugar if desired. **9 servings**

Poppy Seed Filling

⅓ cup poppy seed
⅓ cup walnuts
¼ cup milk
¼ cup honey

Place all ingredients in blender or food processor. Cover and blend on medium speed, stopping blender frequently to scrape sides, or process, until milk is absorbed.

PER SERVING: Calories 410; Protein 7 g; Carbohydrate 53 g; Fat 19 g; Cholesterol 25 mg; Sodium 340 mg

Oatmeal-Plum Coffee Cake

If plums aren't available (or if you just really love pears) substitute 1½ cups chopped fresh pears for the plums. The results are equally delicious!

Streusel Topping (below)
1¾ cups all-purpose flour
1 cup packed brown sugar
¾ cup quick-cooking or regular oats
½ cup (1 stick) margarine or butter, softened
1 cup buttermilk
3 teaspoons baking powder
1 teaspoon ground cinnamon
½ teaspoon baking soda
¼ teaspoon salt
¼ teaspoon ground nutmeg
1 egg
1½ cups chopped fresh plums

Heat oven to 350°. Grease square pan, 9 × 9 × 2 inches. Prepare Streusel Topping; reserve. Beat remaining ingredients except plums in large bowl on low speed 30 seconds. Beat on medium speed 2 minutes, scraping bowl occasionally. Stir in plums. Spread in pan. Sprinkle with Streusel Topping. Bake 50 to 55 minutes or until golden brown and toothpick inserted in center comes out clean. Serve warm or let stand until cool. **9 servings**

Streusel Topping

2 tablespoons firm margarine or butter
¼ cup all-purpose flour
2 tablespoons packed brown sugar
½ teaspoon ground cinnamon
¼ cup quick-cooking or regular oats

Cut margarine into flour, brown sugar and cinnamon until crumbly. Stir in oats.

PER SERVING: Calories 390; Protein 6 g; Carbohydrate 60 g; Fat 14 g; Cholesterol 25 mg; Sodium 430 mg

English Muffin Bread

Cornmeal
2¾ cups all-purpose flour
1 teaspoon salt
1 teaspoon sugar
1 package regular or quick-acting active dry yeast
1 cup very warm water (120° to 130°)
¼ cup shortening

Grease loaf pan, 8½ × 4½ × 2½ or 9 × 5 × 3 inches; coat with cornmeal. Mix 1½ cups of the flour, the salt, sugar and yeast in large bowl. Add warm water and shortening. Beat on low speed 30 seconds, scraping bowl constantly. Beat on high speed 3 minutes, scraping bowl occasionally. Stir in remaining flour. Smooth and pat batter in pan with floured hands. Sprinkle with cornmeal if desired. Cover and let rise in warm place about 45 minutes or until batter is about ¾ inch above top of 8½-inch pan or about ¾ inch below top of 9-inch pan.

Heat oven to 375°. Bake 40 to 45 minutes or until loaf is golden brown and sounds hollow when tapped; remove from pan. Brush with softened margarine or butter if desired. Cool on wire rack. **1 loaf (16 slices)**

PER SERVING: Calories 95; Protein 2 g; Carbohydrate 15 g; Fat 3 g; Cholesterol 0 mg; Sodium 135 mg

Bacon-Corn Bread

Bacon-Corn Bread

1½ cups yellow cornmeal
½ cup all-purpose flour
¼ cup shortening or bacon fat
1½ cups buttermilk
2 teaspoons baking powder
1 teaspoon sugar
½ teaspoon salt
½ teaspoon baking soda
4 slices crisply cooked bacon, crumbled
2 eggs

Heat oven to 450°. Grease round pan, 9 × 1½ inches, or square pan, 8 × 8 × 2 inches. Mix all ingredients; beat vigorously 30 seconds. Pour into pan. Bake 25 to 30 minutes or until golden brown. Serve warm. **12 servings**

BACON-CORN STICKS: Fill 18 greased corn stick pans about seven-eighths full. Bake 12 to 15 minutes.

PER SERVING: Calories 155; Protein 4 g; Carbohydrate 19 g; Fat 7 g; Cholesterol 40 mg; Sodium 260 mg

Fresh Herb Batter Bread

3 cups all-purpose flour
1 tablespoon sugar
1 teaspoon salt
1 package regular or quick-acting active dry yeast
1¼ cups very warm water (120° to 130°)
2 tablespoons chopped fresh parsley
2 tablespoons shortening
1½ teaspoons chopped fresh or ½ teaspoon dried rosemary leaves
½ teaspoon chopped fresh or ¼ teaspoon dried thyme leaves
Margarine or butter, softened

Grease loaf pan, 9 × 5 × 3 inches. Mix 2 cups of the flour, the sugar, salt and yeast in large bowl. Add warm water, parsley, shortening, rosemary and thyme. Beat on low speed 1 minute, scraping bowl frequently. Beat on medium speed 1 minute, scraping bowl frequently. Stir in remaining flour until smooth. Smooth and pat batter in pan with floured hands. Cover and let rise in warm place about 40 minutes or until double.

Heat oven to 375°. Bake 40 to 45 minutes or until loaf sounds hollow when tapped; remove from pan. Brush with margarine. Cool on wire rack. **1 loaf (16 slices)**

PER SERVING: Calories 110; Protein 2 g; Carbohydrate 19 g; Fat 3 g; Cholesterol 0 mg; Sodium 140 mg

Fresh Fruit with French Cream (page 90)

4

Tempting Beverages and Fruit Sides

Grapefruit Juleps

A refreshing, alcohol-free twist on the mint julep.

1 quart grapefruit juice
½ cup fresh lime juice
½ cup chopped fresh mint leaves
¼ cup sugar
2 cups sparkling water, chilled
Fresh mint sprigs

Mix all ingredients except sparkling water and mint sprigs in 2-quart pitcher. Refrigerate 1 hour. Strain mixture to remove chopped mint; mix with sparkling water. Serve in tall glasses with ice; garnish with mint sprigs.   **6 servings**

PER SERVING: Calories 105; Protein 1 g; Carbohydrate 25 g; Fat 0 g; Cholesterol 0 mg; Sodium 10 mg

Strawberry-Orange Juice

8 cups orange juice
1 package (10 ounces) frozen sliced strawberries, thawed

Combine orange juice and strawberries in large pitcher until well blended.   **8 servings**

PER SERVING: Calories 150; Protein 2 g; Carbohydrate 36 g; Fat 0 g; Cholesterol 0 mg; Sodium 5 mg

Beverage Bar

It's important to have a selection of beverages on hand when entertaining, even when you have prepared a specific drink for a menu. Below is a list of beverages to have on hand; it's no problem if they aren't used at the meal—you can always use and enjoy them another time.

- Buy seltzer or club soda (if you usually buy flavored seltzer, be sure to have plain seltzer also on hand).

- Have fruit juices available.

- When serving wine, provide a choice between both red and white, as many people have a decided preference. Be generous when buying wine—count on half a bottle per person. Unopened wine can always be used another day.

- If you serve beer, count on at least two beers per person.

- Offer guests both caffeinated and decaffeinated tea and coffee, as well as herbal tea.

- Have ice on hand.

- Set out lemon and lime wedges—many people enjoy them in seltzer and club soda.

Summer Fruit Coolers

You can make this with or without alcohol—whichever you prefer.

2 tablespoons sugar
1 cup sparkling water
½ cup orange juice
1 bottle (25 ounces) dry white wine or white grape juice
½ cup halved green grapes
1 medium orange, cut into halves and thinly sliced
1 kiwifruit, peeled and sliced

Mix sugar, sparkling water, orange juice and wine in large pitcher. Stir in fruit. Chill for 1 hour. Serve coolers over ice.   **6 servings**

PER SERVING: Calories 140; Protein 1 g; Carbohydrate 15 g; Fat 0 g; Cholesterol 0 mg; Sodium 10 mg

Spring Breeze Punch

Pour sparkling water into punch 1 hour or less before serving—otherwise punch will be flat.

2 cups cold water
1 can (6 ounces) frozen tangerine juice, thawed
1 can (6 ounces) frozen grapefruit juice, thawed
1 bottle (32 ounces) sparkling water

Combine all ingredients. Serve well chilled.

6 servings

PER SERVING: Calories 90; Protein 1 g; Carbohydrate 21 g; Fat 0 g; Cholesterol 0 mg; Sodium 5 mg

Pineapple Limeade

½ cup sugar
3 cups pineapple juice
½ cup lime juice
1 quart sparkling water, chilled

Mix all ingredients except sparkling water; refrigerate until chilled. Just before serving; stir in sparkling water. Serve over ice. Garnish with lime slices if desired. **8 servings**

PER SERVING: Calories 105; Protein 0 g; Carbohydrate 26 g; Fat 0 g; Cholesterol 0 mg; Sodium 5 mg

Hot Spiced Cider

A wonderfully warming drink on a chilly day!

10 cups apple cider
1 teaspoon whole cloves
½ teaspoon ground nutmeg
6 sticks cinnamon

Heat all ingredients to boiling in large saucepan over medium-high heat; reduce heat and simmer 10 minutes. Strain to remove whole spices. Keep hot. **10 servings**

PER SERVING: Calories 115; Protein 0 g; Carbohydrate 29 g; Fat 0 g; Cholesterol 0 mg; Sodium 10 mg

Café au Lait

This French recipe makes coffee that is mild and mellow.

4½ cups strong coffee
4½ cups hot milk

Pour equal amounts of hot coffee and hot milk simultaneously from separate pots into each cup. **12 servings**

PER SERVING: Calories 50; Protein 3 g; Carbohydrate 5 g; Fat 2 g; Cholesterol 5 mg; Sodium 45 mg

Orange Café au Lait

½ cup powdered nondairy creamer
½ cup sugar
¼ cup freeze-dried instant coffee
1 teaspoon dried orange peel
¼ teaspoon ground cinnamon

Place all ingredients in blender or food processor. Cover and blend on high speed 30 seconds, stopping blender after 15 seconds to stir, or process 5 to 10 seconds or until well mixed. Store in tightly covered container at room temperature no longer than 6 months.

For each serving, place 2 teaspoons mix in cup. Add ⅔ cup boiling water. For 6 servings, place ¼ cup mix in heatproof container and add 4 cups boiling water. **24 servings**

DESSERT ORANGE CAFÉ AU LAIT: Stir 1 tablespoon orange-flavored liqueur into each serving and top with whipped cream.

40 calories per serving

PER SERVING: Calories 30; Protein 0 g; Carbohydrate 5 g; Fat 1 g; Cholesterol 0 mg; Sodium 5 mg

International Coffee

1 cup instant cocoa mix
¾ cup instant coffee
12 cups boiling water
Sweetened whipped cream

Mix cocoa and coffee in a large serving pot. Pour in boiling water; stir. Serve steaming hot and top with whipped cream.   **12 servings**

PER SERVING: Calories 60; Protein 0 g; Carbohydrate 11 g; Fat 2 g; Cholesterol 0 mg; Sodium 50 mg

Café Mexicano

8 cups cold water
½ cup grated piloncillo or ⅓ cup packed dark brown sugar
½ ounce unsweetened chocolate, finely chopped
2 whole cloves
1 stick cinnamon, broken into halves
1 cup regular-grind coffee (dry)
1 teaspoon vanilla

Heat water, piloncillo, chocolate, cloves, and cinnamon to boiling in 3-quart saucepan; reduce heat. Simmer uncovered 15 minutes.

Stir in coffee. Remove from heat; cover and let stand 5 minutes. Stir in vanilla. Strain coffee through 4 thicknesses cheesecloth.

7 servings

PER SERVING: Calories 70; Protein 1 g; Carbohydrate 14 g; Fat 1 g; Cholesterol 0 mg; Sodium 10 mg

Fiesta Hot Chocolate

½ cup cocoa
1 tablespoon all-purpose flour
⅓ cup grated piloncillo or ¼ cup packed dark brown sugar
4 cups milk
3 whole cloves
1 stick cinnamon, broken into halves
2 tablespoons powdered sugar
1½ teaspoons vanilla
Whipped cream
4 sticks cinnamon

Mix cocoa and flour in 2-quart saucepan. Stir in piloncillo, milk, cloves and 1 stick cinnamon. Heat just to boiling over medium heat, stirring constantly; reduce heat. Simmer uncovered 5 minutes (do not boil). Remove from heat; remove cloves and cinnamon. Stir in powdered sugar and vanilla.

Beat with molinillo, wire whisk or hand beater until foamy. Pour into 4 cups or mugs. Serve with whipped cream and cinnamon sticks.

4 servings

PER SERVING: Calories 285; Protein 9 g; Carbohydrate 47 g; Fat 17 g; Cholesterol 20 mg; Sodium 200 mg

Fiesta Hot Chocolate

Coffee Tips

The best coffee is made from fresh-roasted coffee beans, preferably ground just before brewing. The strength of coffee depends directly on the ratio of coffee to water when brewing. Many coffees are blended, a combination of different beans, lighter and darker roasts, and even beans of varying quality. From whole beans to flaked coffee, the selection of flavors and grinds is vast.

• Regular grind is an intermediate grind size used in automatic percolator-type coffee makers and range-top percolators. As the water boils, it continually washes through the ground coffee.

• Drip or fine grind is used in drip coffee makers and espresso machines in which the water passes through the ground coffee only once.

• Electric perk and flaked are designed especially for electric percolators and automatic drip coffee makers.

Store whole beans and ground coffee in airtight containers in the freezer to slow oxidation and loss of flavor. Because coffee is naturally oily, freezing will keep it from becoming rancid. Store for six months in the freezer or for a month in the refrigerator.

Easy Fruit Salad

1 can (20 ounces) pineapple chunks, drained, and 2 tablespoons juice reserved
1 can (17 ounces) apricot halves, drained
1 can (16 ounces) pitted red tart cherries, drained
1 can (11 ounces) mandarin orange segments, drained
1 cup miniature marshmallows
Fruit Salad Dressing (below)

Mix pineapple, apricots, cherries, orange segments and marshmallows. Toss with Fruit Salad Dressing. Cover and refrigerate at least 12 hours. **8 servings**

Fruit Salad Dressing

1 cup whipping (heavy) cream
2 tablespoons reserved pineapple juice
Dash of salt

Beat whipping cream in chilled bowl on high speed until soft peaks form. Stir in remaining ingredients.

PER SERVING: Calories 165; Protein 1 g; Carbohydrate 37 g; Fat 2 g; Cholesterol 0 mg; Sodium 20 mg

Zesty Fruit Salad

1 cup strawberries, cut into halves
1 medium papaya, peeled, seeded and
    cut into 1-inch pieces (about 2 cups)
1 kiwifruit, pared and thinly sliced
1 starfruit, thinly sliced and seeded
Jalapeño Dressing (below)

Toss all ingredients. Serve on salad greens if
desired.   **4 servings**

Jalapeño Dressing

1 tablespoon chopped fresh cilantro
    leaves
1 tablespoon vegetable oil
1 tablespoon lime juice
1 teaspoon sugar
½ small jalapeño chile, seeded and very
    finely chopped

Mix all ingredients.

PER SERVING: Calories 105; Protein 1 g; Carbohydrate 17 g; Fat 4 g; Cholesterol 0 mg; Sodium 5 mg

Tropical Salad

2 papayas or mangoes, pared and cubed
    (about 2 cups)
1 cup sliced strawberries
1 cup cubed pineapple*
1 kiwifruit, pared and sliced
2 tablespoons frozen (thawed) limeade
    concentrate
1 tablespoon vegetable oil
1 tablespoon honey
⅛ teaspoon poppy seed

Mix fruit in bowl. Shake remaining ingredients
in tightly covered container. Pour over fruit and
toss.   **6 servings**

*1 can (8 ounces) pineapple chunks, drained, can be substi-
tuted for the fresh pineapple.

PER SERVING: Calories 90; Protein 1 g; Carbohydrate 17 g; Fat 3 g; Cholesterol 0 mg; Sodium 5 mg

Ambrosia Fruit Salad

Ambrosia Fruit Salad

Although myriad variations exist, this heavenly salad or dessert always contains oranges and coconut. It is best served icy cold. Ambrosia was the food of the Greek gods.

1 large grapefruit, pared and sectioned
3 medium oranges, pared and sectioned
½ cup seedless green grape halves
1 to 2 tablespoons light corn syrup
1 tablespoon dry sherry, if desired
1 large banana, sliced
¼ cup flaked coconut

Cut grapefruit sections into halves. Mix grapefruit, oranges, grapes, corn syrup and sherry. Cover and refrigerate at least 2 hours but no longer than 24 hours. Stir in banana and coconut just before serving.　　**6 servings**

PER SERVING: Calories 115; Protein 1 g; Carbohydrate 25 g; Fat 1 g; Cholesterol 0 mg; Sodium 15 mg

Ripe and Ready

An easy guide to buying tropical fruits.

- Bananas ripen better off the plant than on it. Select slightly green fruit and allow to mature as a cheerful centerpiece. When you think the ripening has gone far enough, refrigerate. The skins may blacken, but the flesh will keep for several days.

- The egg-shaped kiwifruit hides a luscious green under its drab brown exterior. Let ripen at room temperature until soft, then refrigerate. Once peeled, the whole fruit is edible.

- Mangoes vary in size and shape. Allow them to ripen at room temperature until the flesh yields to gentle pressure and any green is largely background color, then refrigerate. To prepare, score the tough skin in 4 to 6 sections, piercing it with a paring knife; strip the skin away and cut the fruit into slices.

- Papayas look like pear-shaped melons, but they grow on trees, not vines. If purchased when green, let ripen at room temperature for 3 to 5 days. When yellow-orange, refrigerate for use within 1 week. Prepare and serve just as you would cantaloupe.

- Pineapples don't ripen after picking. Try for one that has an aroma, no soft spots and a spirited green crown. Refrigerate if not using immediately. To prepare a pineapple for use, carefully twist out the green top; cut pineapple into halves, then quarters. Slice the fruit from the rind. Cut off the core and remove any "eyes."

Warm Banana and Papaya Salad

Passion fruit is an "ugly duckling" fruit with a leathery, brown skin that has a wrinkled appearance when ripe. The fruit inside is tangy and sweet with dark, edible seeds.

1 passion fruit
1 tablespoon sugar
2 tablespoons margarine or butter
2 small bananas or 1 plantain, cut into ¼-inch slices
1 papaya, pared and cut into ¼-inch slices, or 1 small cantaloupe, cut into ¼-inch slices
¼ cup sweet white wine or apple juice

Cut passion fruit crosswise into halves. Scoop pulp and seeds into bowl; discard skin. Heat sugar and margarine in 10-inch skillet over medium-high heat until margarine is melted. Stir in bananas and papaya. Heat about 2 minutes or until warm. Remove to plate; keep warm.

Add wine to skillet. Heat to boiling. Cook about 2 minutes or until reduced slightly. Stir in passion fruit; heat until hot. Serve over bananas and papaya.   **4 servings**

PER SERVING: Calories 145; Protein 1 g; Carbohydrate 24 g; Fat 6 g; Cholesterol 0 mg; Sodium 70 mg

Waldorf Salad

2 medium apples, coarsely chopped (about 2 cups)
2 medium stalks celery, chopped (about 1 cup)
½ cup mayonnaise or salad dressing
⅓ cup coarsely chopped nuts

Toss all ingredients. Serve on salad greens if desired.   **4 servings**

PEAR WALDORF SALAD: Substitute 4 pears, coarsely chopped, for the apples.

WALDORF SALAD SUPREME: Decrease celery to 1 medium stalk and nuts to ¼ cup. Stir in 1 can (8 ounces) pineapple chunks, drained, ½ cup miniature marshmallows and ⅓ cup chopped dates.

PER SERVING: Calories 310; Protein 2 g; Carbohydrate 14 g; Fat 28 g; Cholesterol 0 mg; Sodium 75 mg

Waldorf Salad, Tropical Salad (page 79), and Melon and Fig Salad (page 89)

Two-Pear Waldorf Salad

The most common variety of Asian pear is large, round, yellow-green and sweeter and crunchier than an ordinary pear. If Asian pears aren't to be found, substitute an apple or another Bosc pear.

⅓ cup plain lowfat yogurt
1 tablespoon cholesterol-free reduced-
    calorie mayonnaise or salad dressing
½ teaspoon finely grated lime peel
1 teaspoon lime juice
½ cup sliced celery (about 1 stalk)
½ cup seedless red grape halves
2 tablespoons chopped walnuts
1 Bosc or Anjou pear, coarsely chopped
1 Asian pear, coarsely chopped

Mix yogurt, mayonnaise, lime peel and lime juice. Toss with remaining ingredients.

4 servings

PER SERVING: Calories 105; Protein 2 g; Carbohydrate 18 g; Fat 4 g; Cholesterol 1 mg; Sodium 50 mg

Kiwifruit Salad

An unusual and very pleasant mixture of kiwifruit, avocado and champagne vinegar make for a memorable salad.

Champagne Vinegar Dressing (below)
1 small bunch romaine lettuce, torn into
    bite-size pieces (about 10 cups)
1 avocado, peeled, pitted and sliced
3 kiwifruit, peeled and sliced

Prepare Champagne Vinegar Dressing. Place lettuce in salad bowl; top with avocado and kiwifruit. Drizzle with dressing. **8 servings**

Champagne Vinegar Dressing

½ cup champagne vinegar
¼ cup vegetable oil
1 tablespoon sugar
1 tablespoon Dijon mustard

Shake all ingredients in tightly covered jar until well blended.

PER SERVING: Calories 130; Protein 1 g; Carbohydrate 9 g; Fat 10 g; Cholesterol 0 mg; Sodium 30 mg

Pear and Blue Cheese Salad

Romaine lettuce leaves
2 red pears, cored and thinly sliced
2 green pears, cored and thinly sliced
½ cup crumbled blue cheese
Cider Vinaigrette (below)

Arrange lettuce leaves on each of 8 salad plates. Divide red and green pear slices evenly among plates; top each salad with about 1 tablespoon blue cheese. Drizzle each salad with about 2 tablespoons Cider Vinaigrette.

8 servings

Cider Vinaigrette

½ cup light olive oil or vegetable oil
2 tablespoons cider vinegar
1 teaspoon Dijon mustard
¼ teaspoon salt
¼ teaspoon pepper

Shake all ingredients in tightly covered container.

PER SERVING: Calories 210; Protein 2 g; Carbohydrate 14 g; Fat 16 g; Cholesterol 5 mg; Sodium 190 mg

Pineapple Salad

This fresh pineapple salad is drenched with the sweet-salty flavor that is found in Thai cuisine.

⅓ cup olive or vegetable oil
2 tablespoons lemon juice
1 tablespoon soy sauce
1 to 2 teaspoons packed brown sugar
1 small pineapple
1 tart red apple, diced
3 green onions (with tops), sliced
1 small bunch romaine, shredded

Shake oil, lemon juice, soy sauce and brown sugar in tightly covered jar. Cut top off pineapple; cut pineapple into fourths. Cut fruit from rind; remove core and any "eyes." Slice each fourth lengthwise; cut crosswise into chunks.

Toss pineapple chunks, apple and green onions with dressing. Place romaine in shallow bowl; mound fruit mixture in center. **6 servings**

PER SERVING: Calories 180; Protein 1 g; Carbohydrate 17 g; Fat 12 g; Cholesterol 0 mg; Sodium 180 mg

Orange Salad with Pecan Dressing

4 oranges, pared
1 head lettuce, torn into bite-size pieces
Pecan Dressing (below)

Cut oranges crosswise into slices; cut slices into fourths. Mix oranges and lettuce. Toss with Pecan Dressing. **6 servings**

Pecan Dressing

¼ cup ground pecans
2 tablespoons mayonnaise or salad dressing
2 tablespoons sour cream
1 tablespoon lime juice
½ teaspoon sugar
½ teaspoon salt
⅛ teaspoon ground cinnamon
Dash of pepper

Mix all ingredients.

PER SERVING: Calories 115; Protein 1 g; Carbohydrate 12 g; Fat 7 g; Cholesterol 5 mg; Sodium 210 mg

Jicama-Citrus Salad with Sangria Dressing

3 large oranges, pared and sectioned
2 red grapefruit, pared and sectioned
1 medium jicama (about 1 pound), pared and cut into ½-inch cubes
Sangria Dressing (below)

Arrange oranges, grapefruit and jicama on 8 salad plates or mix together. Serve with Sangria Dressing. **8 servings**

Sangria Dressing

¼ cup vegetable oil
¼ cup dry red wine
2 tablespoons honey
2 tablespoons orange juice

Shake all ingredients in tightly covered container.

PER SERVING: Calories 175; Protein 2 g; Carbohydrate 26 g; Fat 7 g; Cholesterol 0 mg; Sodium 10 mg

Jicama-Citrus Salad

Rio Grande Melon Salad

Broiled Honey Grapefruit

A simple dish that adds welcome flavor to any breakfast.

2 grapefruits, cut into halves
¼ cup honey
8 to 10 drops aromatic bitters or ½ teaspoon lemon juice, if desired

Remove seeds from grapefruit halves. Cut around edges and sections to loosen; remove centers. Mix honey and bitters; spoon about 1 tablespoon honey mixture over each grapefruit half.

Set oven control to broil. Broil grapefruit halves with tops 5 inches from heat about 5 minutes. **4 servings**

PER SERVING: Calories 120; Protein 1 g; Carbohydrate 29 g; Fat 0 g; Cholesterol 0 mg; Sodium 5 mg

Melon and Fig Salad

2 cups melon balls or cubes
4 fresh or 8 dried figs, cut into fourths
⅓ cup bottled poppy seed dressing
Bibb lettuce leaves

Mix fruit and poppy seed dressing. Serve on 4 lettuce-lined plates. **4 servings**

PER SERVING: Calories 220; Protein 1 g; Carbohydrate 30 g; Fat 12 g; Cholesterol 0 mg; Sodium 120 mg

Rio Grande Melon Salad

2 cups watermelon balls
2 mangoes or papayas, pared and sliced
½ honeydew melon, pared, seeded and thinly sliced
¾ cup seedless red grape halves
1 large bunch watercress
Honey-Lime Dressing (below)

Arrange fruits on watercress. Drizzle with Honey-Lime Dressing. **6 servings**

Honey-Lime Dressing

⅓ cup vegetable oil
¼ teaspoon grated lime peel
2 tablespoons lime juice
1 tablespoon honey

Shake all ingredients in tightly covered container.

PER SERVING: Calories 250; Protein 1 g; Carbohydrate 32 g; Fat 13 g; Cholesterol 0 mg; Sodium 20 mg

Winter Fruit Salad with Honey Dressing

Make this salad ahead of time, if you like, and drizzle with dressing just before serving.

Honey Dressing (below)
2 tangerines, peeled and sectioned
2 apples, peeled, cored and sliced
2 bananas, peeled and sliced
1 kiwifruit, peeled and sliced

Prepare Honey Dressing. Divide fruit evenly among 8 salad plates; arrange fruit on plates. Drizzle with Honey Dressing.   **8 servings**

Honey Dressing

⅓ cup lemon juice
⅓ cup vegetable oil
⅓ cup honey
⅛ teaspoon ground ginger

Shake all ingredients in tightly covered container.

PER SERVING: Calories 190; Protein 0 g; Carbohydrate 27 g; Fat 9 g; Cholesterol 0 mg; Sodium 5 mg

Fresh Fruit with French Cream

French crème fraîche is something like sour cream but less acid or "soured" tasting. The sauce below is our quick version.

⅔ cup whipping cream
⅓ cup sour cream
2 to 3 cups assorted fresh fruit (see Note)
Ground nutmeg or sugar

Gradually stir whipping cream into sour cream. Cover and refrigerate no longer than 48 hours. Serve over fruit. Sprinkle with nutmeg.
     4 to 6 servings

NOTE: Suggested fruits are blueberries, raspberries, strawberries, sliced peaches or cubed pineapple.

PER SERVING: Calories 195; Protein 2 g; Carbohydrate 11 g; Fat 16 g; Cholesterol 55 mg; Sodium 25 mg

Spicy Fruit Compote

This compote is a nice side dish for meat, or to serve on its own as a refreshing end to the meal.

1 two-inch cinnamon stick
6 whole cloves
¼ cup sugar
½ cup port, sweet red wine or apple juice
½ cup water
2 tablespoons lemon juice
1 package (11 ounces) mixed dried fruit
2 bananas, sliced

Tie cinnamon stick and cloves in cheesecloth bag. Heat cheesecloth bag, sugar, port, water and lemon juice to boiling in 2-quart saucepan. Stir in dried fruit. Heat to boiling; reduce heat.

Simmer uncovered 10 to 15 minutes, stirring occasionally, until fruit is plump and tender. Refrigerate uncovered about 3 hours, stirring occasionally, until chilled.

Remove cheesecloth bag. Stir bananas into fruit mixture until coated with syrup. Drain fruit, reserving syrup. Serve fruit with some of the syrup. Serve with sour cream or plain yogurt if desired. **6 servings**

PER SERVING: Calories 220; Protein 1 g; Carbohydrate 58 g; Fat 0 g; Cholesterol 0 mg; Sodium 10 mg

METRIC CONVERSION GUIDE

U.S. UNITS	CANADIAN METRIC	AUSTRALIAN METRIC
Volume		
1/4 teaspoon	1 mL	1 ml
1/2 teaspoon	2 mL	2 ml
1 teaspoon	5 mL	5 ml
1 tablespoon	15 mL	20 ml
1/4 cup	50 mL	60 ml
1/3 cup	75 mL	80 ml
1/2 cup	125 mL	125 ml
2/3 cup	150 mL	170 ml
3/4 cup	175 mL	190 ml
1 cup	250 mL	250 ml
1 quart	1 liter	1 liter
1 1/2 quarts	1.5 liter	1.5 liter
2 quarts	2 liters	2 liters
2 1/2 quarts	2.5 liters	2.5 liters
3 quarts	3 liters	3 liters
4 quarts	4 liters	4 liters
Weight		
1 ounce	30 grams	30 grams
2 ounces	55 grams	60 grams
3 ounces	85 grams	90 grams
4 ounces (1/4 pound)	115 grams	125 grams
8 ounces (1/2 pound)	225 grams	225 grams
16 ounces (1 pound)	455 grams	500 grams
1 pound	455 grams	1/2 kilogram

Measurements

Inches	Centimeters
1	2.5
2	5.0
3	7.5
4	10.0
5	12.5
6	15.0
7	17.5
8	20.5
9	23.0
10	25.5
11	28.0
12	30.5
13	33.0
14	35.5
15	38.0

Temperatures

Fahrenheit	Celsius
32°	0°
212°	100°
250°	120°
275°	140°
300°	150°
325°	160°
350°	180°
375°	190°
400°	200°
425°	220°
450°	230°
475°	240°
500°	260°

NOTE
The recipes in this cookbook have not been developed or tested using metric measures. When converting recipes to metric, some variations in quality may be noted.

Index